Bhagavad Gita and Hinduism
What Everyone should Know

About the Author

Nilesh M. Shukla (b.1951), an engineer by profession, has worked in some leading organizations in India and abroad including Bhabha Atomic Research Centre. He took early retirement from active jobs to pursue his other interests. His areas of interest include philosophy, history and geography. He has to his credit a number of articles and research papers published in various journals of repute. He is very impressed with the Swadhyaya Movement, spearheaded by Pandurang Shashtri Athavale.

Bhagavad Gita and Hinduism
What Everyone should Know

Nilesh M. Shukla

Readworthy
New Delhi

First published 2010

Readworthy Publications (P) Ltd.

Regd. Off
A-18, Mohan Garden
Near Nawada Metro Station
New Delhi – 110 059-06
Phone: 011-2537 1324
Fax: +91-11-2537 1323

Branch
4735/22, Prakash Deep Building,
Ground Floor, Ansari Road, Daryaganj
New Delhi–110 002-02
Phone: 011-4354 9197
Fax: +91-11-2324 3060

Email: info@readworthypub.com
Web: www.readworthypub.com

Cataloging in Publication Data--DK
Courtesy: D.K. Agencies (P) Ltd. <docinfo@dkagencies.com>

Shukla, Nilesh M., 1951-
Bhagavad Gita and Hinduism : what everyone should know / Nilesh M. Shukla.
p. cm.
Includes bibliographical references.
Includes index.

ISBN 13: 978-93-80009-66-7 ISBN 10: 93-80009-66-6

1. Bhagavadgītā--Criticism, interpretation, etc. 2. Hinduism. I. Title.

DDC 294.5924046 22

Printed at Salasar Imaging Systems, Delhi - 35

Preface

Certain important aspects of Hinduism and the Bhagavad Gita that have remained less-exposed are brought to light in this work; some known, some lesser known and some new, along with English translation of the Bhagavad Gita. Intended for a general audience, the book attempts to provide a non-academic exposition of the Bhagavad Gita and Hinduism by conveying its spirit to the casual reader in short, in simple and largely jargon-free language, presenting connections (and contradictions). Notwithstanding large knowledge-pool of this oriental knowledge, I consider it more important to connect its value to human progress; reduction in societal problems and the individual growth instead of traversing beaten path of merely presenting information covering this timeless philosophy.

Hinduism and the Bhagavad Gita are not difficult to understand, however, most literatures available today suffer from the flaw of triple-distillation. All the translations across the world naturally do suffer from certain erosion from their original spirit and they cannot be faulted for that. However, in this case, a further factor is in play; there simply are no equivalent Western words corresponding to several key terms that make core of the Hindu philosophy. Those terms and ideas such as 'Yajna', Tyaag', 'Punya', 'Samarpan' et cetera were translated using nearest available European terms and were explained in European languages that intrinsically did not have many of those ideas. Sanskrit 'Pinda' when translated as 'ball of rice' could hardly provide meaningful understanding, although 'it indeed is prepared from boiled rice. Whatever European terms were deployed had their own original meanings in their own languages which on ocassions led its readers, who became subsequent translators and writers, to arrive at different meanings than the one intended by its first generation translators, even giving them a benefit of doubt that they did understand true spirit contained in the original. Those readers who became second, third or subsequent translators are the ones whose translations and commentaries are read by us and we are left to uncover the real meanings behind the maze of inaccuracies. An attempt is made here to make for more meaningful reading by bringing to light certain unique ideas that, I felt, are lost in translation.

Since the book has a fair amount of preparatory background information, especially on the basics of Hinduism; how a Hindu mind is made up; and a separate section about what the reader should look for while reading the Gita, it enables the reader to focus on the essential message of the ancient text rather than being distracted with relevant but not necessarily essential information. Before it goes into the original Sanskrit text and its translation, reader is led through the Gita's position in Hindu literature. In the end, a section deals with what messages mankind can derive, for personal evolution as well as for society's good, everything centering around action that a man himself can and should take instead of just prayers awaiting "God's will".

I must also confess at the very outset that this work does not claim to be a treatise or an all-encompassing work either on the Gita or on Hinduism. Freedom to interpret is integral to Hinduism and is allowed to every individual, thereby creating thousands of streams or schools of thought. This book represents but one of them. And true to its title this book is not "everything about the Bhagavad Gita and Hinduism" but it is about "what everyone should know about these two". Further, it would not be proper to say that this book is 'on' the Bhagavad Gita and Hinduism, for I believe only a select few have the capability of writing 'on' these and I am not certainly one of them.

The inspiration to treat the subject in a completely different manner than done conventionally has come to me from Verse 67 of the last chapter of the Gita. The verse implies that the reader of this knowledge will not benefit unless he has a keen desire to know, and is devoted to learning. In deference to this verse, I have attempted to first sow the seeds of a keener curiosity in the mind of the reader about the Bhagavad Gita and the truths that it treats, before stepping into the translation.

I would advise those, who have a serious interest in the Bhagavad Gita, to learn from a good master by listening (rather than reading) for more accurate and more comprehensive knowledge on the subject. Believe it or not, despite all the available literature on the Gita, including this book, there simply is no substitute to learning from the master, sitting at his feet. Even Gita tells the same at 4-34: "Acquire this transcendental knowledge from a Self-realized master by humble reverence, by sincere inquiry, and by service. The empowered ones, who have realized the Truth, will teach you."

This book may well serve as a general guide to students to get a quick snapshot of Hinduism and the Bhagavad Gita, what has been otherwise made out to be a very daunting reading. A complete translation in English, along with original text in Sanskrit will make this material a good reference book.

The major objective of the book is to let people know that it is not difficult to read and understand the Gita and then to check if its knowledge could change the way we look at the world and if this knowledge is found to be that important, should we just sit back, doing nothing, letting the world continue on its path to self-destruct? Would we not check out, what we, the citizens of this world, have inherited from our very thoughtful ancestors?

I want to single out, for special mention, besides the innumerable valued mentors, friends, philosophers and guides, to whom I am thankful, the one whom I consider to be the most brilliant thinker of our times, the revered Pandurang

Shashtri Athavale[1] (1920-2003), a recipient of 1997 Templeton Prize[2]. Using nothing else but the revelations of the Gita, he spearheaded the global phenomena of 'Swadhyay' (Translated: 'Study of the Self'), an activity that has made a cultural revolution by reinforcing human dignity among the participants. As the Swadhyay activity[3] is done without much ado, it was described by Mr. Majid Rehnuma[4] as a 'silent but singing revolution'. Also, I profusely thank Mr. Sanjay Prasad of International Gita Society[5] for graciously permitting me to use the English translation of the Bhagavad Gita, done by his father Dr. Ram Prasad. And indeed it would be unthinkable to have accomplished my task without support and help from my wife, Purnima, my daughter Unnati, her husband Zubin, my son Nipun and his wife Mittal; my task became everyone's concern.

---

1 Mr. Pandurang Shashtri Athavale, Saintly-Philosopher (1920-2001), Creator of a movement known as "Swadhyay" which has a large following. This group is known as Swadhyay Parivar' (translated 'a family engaged in the study-of-the-self'), and is responsible for sea-changes in the lives of millions of fishermen, farmers, forest dwellers as much as urban elites. He was awarded several prestigious awards including the Templeton, Padma Vibhushan and Magsaysay.

2 John Templeton Foundation honors distinguished philosophers with the world's richest prize (bigger than Nobel Prize in its monetary value). For 1997 prize, the nomination was done by Betty Miller Unterberg, Prof of History at Texas A&M University.

3 Inspired by revered Pandurang Shashtri Athavale, the Swadhyay activity is now spread to all the five continents, with literally millions indulging in self-less service and human uplifting. Most major cities of the world would have some or the other Swadhyay activity related to study-of-the-self. Some details of the activity can be seen at www.swadhyay.org. After his death, currently the activity is ably guided by his adopted daughter Mrs. Jayshree Talvalkar.

4 Mr. Majid Rehnuma: Thinker, Iranian Career Diplomat, UN office bearer, opted for career as educator and held teaching positions at Stanford, Harvard, Berkeley and Pennsylvania Universities.

5 International Gita society is one of the few dedicated organizations that are actively promoting reading and studies of the Bhagavad Gita. More details can be had from www.Gita-Society.com

Contents

1

Introduction

Religion is a bad word. Tony Blair, a deeply religious man, could openly talk about his religious convictions only after he relinquished British prime ministership. He explained that in a BBC documentary:[6] "You talk about it in our system and frankly, people do think you are a nutter". Religion has a pejorative connotation for many reasons. Religion divides people, promotes intolerance, inflicts atrocities, compels code of conduct, spreads superstition and exhibits irrational behaviour. It has killed more people than any other single cause. With rising religious terrorism, it is considered by many world thinkers as the biggest threat. Religion seems to possess a deadly sting and a hinderance on the path towards spirituality. Surely this could not be the idea behind religion.

In the world that is fragmented on religious, ethnic, linguistic, race, castes and class lines, the timeless Bhagavad Gita and Sanatan Dharma's (Hinduism) idea of the unity of mankind not only makes fascinating reading, but upon reading, it will appear even more fascinating to see how easy it is to employ this knowledge for everyone's good. Gita is nothing else but a book of that knowledge which tells us that we all humans are unconditionally one; nay even the animals, plants and inanimate objects are somehow all connected. Gita is perhaps the only refuge for us to reclaim global peace, progress and prosperity.

---

6 "The Blair Years" BBC1 Broadcast on 25 November 2007.

Uniquely Different or Differently Unique?

I am unique, you are unique, we individuals are all unique. Aren't we?

Our faces are different, skins are different, minds are different and surely our finger-prints are different.

Aren't they?

I live in east, you in west, he in north and she lives in south.

Don't we live differently?

He likes steak, she likes pizza, I like shawarma and you like noodles. Our tastes are different, aren't they?

Together we are a colorful rainbow.

I am Hindu, he is Muslim, she is Christian and they are atheists.

Why can't we all keep our different religions? Surely we should.

But;

I see, I hear, I laugh, I love and I cry no different than you and they. Ultimately aren't we one?

How about one rainbow-religion that holds together all the rainbow people? An all inclusive, not merely accepting all but embracing all?

Prayer to Bhagavan, God or Allah does it not go to the one single Supreme Being?

What else is the Sanatan Dharma but a rainbow religion for rainbow of peoples?

We, the people on this planet, are all individuals with our own unique mind and choices. Different are our ideas, appearances, likes and dislikes, and requirements. No two faces are identical, nor are our fingerprints. Is it then fair to impose a uniform method of worship on everyone? Many may not approve of 'original sin' of Bible and many would disapprove of 'eye-for-eye' justice of Judaism. Many will not agree to publicly beheading or stoning to death as specified in Koran and Hadith, and many would be opposed to idol worship of Hinduism. Many of us are such that even for agreable stuff, we would revolt if it is imposed on us.

Intelligent and sensitive thinkers would perhaps see it as coercion to impose a certain 'God' or deity or system on the entire human race. They would perhaps see the efforts and investments of religious proselytizers as misplaced enthusiasm and abused charity. A serious question needs a serious answer. Should the entire world follow one-single religion; single method of worship? Casting everyone into one mould, isn't it like turning humans into Cola cans and sending them to the filling-plant of church, mosque or temple? Even if done, would it work? Has it worked? Already there are dozens of kinds of Christians who have evolved from one Christianity and so is the case with several sects of Muslims and hundreds of kinds of Hindus owing to differences inherent to humans. There would always exist different methods of worship. Earlier we accept this truth faster we can reach the solution.

And even if we assume that evangelizers have succeeded in turning everyone into Cola cans, when the entire world has been evangelized to one religion and only one method of worship, would that end problems of the mankind? If the answer is no, why is this effort and investment on proselytizing by the leading religions of the world? What is the plan beyond the horizon of proselytizing? Religiously monolithic countries have much bigger moral, social and spiritul issues than other countries and there seems to have no plan to work where it is really needed; instead they are after harvesting new souls from yet unevangelized countries.

Today's model of marketing faiths erodes morals and divinity of the perpetrator. Because, to succeed and succeed faster, they have to devise cleverer means of giving their message, they have to become competitive; they have to look good and sexual abuse or child molestation, even if present, should be hidden or at worst defended. They have to have more means; millions are not enough, billions are required. Funds must be generated, must be kept safe and growing. Who cares if that brings in with it greed, cheat, cruelity and favoritism in the minds of captains of the religions?

Fair-minded people wonder as to what is happening to the very institutions that are supposed to safeguard our morals. St Paul (AD 364), in his book 'Romans' at 3:7-8, said: "But what if my untruth serves God's glory by making his truth stand out more clearly? Why should I still be condemned as a sinner?" Clearly intent on speaking untruth to 'enhance' the glory of his God! The religions have become fierce battlefields. Everything is fair in war. But, is it?

For the good of the world, all the mainstream religions will have to eventually give up converting others into their fold. Eventually, they would have to teach their followers to accept people of other streams. If and when thinkers of the world were to sit together on the task of forming a common code of conduct or a 'religion' for the whole mankind, a sort of 'Universal-Religion' what would be their thinking? Perhaps they need to think out of the book oops box.

We want peace, progress and prosperity. We want to be one. If one thinks of unity in diversity, where else can one go if not to the Bhagavad Gita? Recall Nobel recipient Hermann Hesse, who explained his poem, entitled Bhagavad Gita. He said: "I tried to discover that which is common to all confessions and all human forms of religiousness and that which stands above all national differences, that which can be believed in and respected by all races". He said: "For me the first dogma is the unity behind and above the opposites". He gives words to our thoughts.

The Gita shows the way, equally to an atheist, to a scientist, to a Christian, to a Muslim, to an educated or uneducated, to the poor or the rich, to sick or healthy, to a ruler or a ruled. The Sanatan Dharma is unique; as it can say and convince us with equal ease that Lord Krishna, Prophet Mohammed or Jesus Christ; all belong to us, one people, people of the world and that they all are divine. If we can appreciate this, separation on religious lines; Semitics ('people of the book'-Jew-Christian-Muslim) on one side and Sanatanis on the other; Christians from Muslims; Jews from Muslims, devouts from kafirs etc. will not occur.

'Universal Religion', where a Christian tries to become a better individual, keeping his Christianity, a Muslim a better individual, keeping his Islam, a Hindu a better individual, remaining a Hindu, a Jew a better individual keeping his Judaism, an atheist a better individual still remaining an atheist, and where no one needs to spread his own 'ism' by degrading other fellow humans. It is more important to become better than to just speak better; more important to purify his inner-self rather than just dress well. What else can be its description except "Sanatan Dharma".

The Gita, a part of the world's heritage, has been called the holy book of Hindus, which it is indeed, and perhaps the sacred-most, but not in the same sense as the Bible is to Christians or the Koran to Muslims. Belief in Bible or in Koran is conditional to being a Christian or a Muslim but belief in the Gita is not a condition placed on Hindus to claim to be a Hindu. A Hindu has the freedom whether to or not to or partially to believe in the Gita. It is this freedom that it grants and its content that has brought the respect to the Gita by a much wider audience than Hindus alone, and is held by many others as a holy book for all mankind. It is essentially a non-sectarian and yet a very sacred text. Further, it is not about prayers, miracles or myths. There is neither any commandment in it, nor any blessing from God. It does not even give moral sermons or explain complicated rituals. It deals only with freedom, developing one's self so as to reach one's goals and a fulfilled state of being. It explains the art of liberating one's self from one's limitations; imaginary or real. And thus, the Gita is universally acceptable and many admirable commentaries have been written on it by authors following different religions from around the world. The sacredness of the Gita comes from the matter in its content and the character of its revealer.

Although in existence for several millennia, the Bhagavad Gita has come to be known to the much of the audience outside India relatively recently. It was first translated in English as late as in 1785 by Sir Charles Wilkins at the instance of the then Governor-General of British India, Warren Hastings, and was only known to a few keen Orientalists. However, owing to its profound philosophical value, many western philosophers were quickly drawn to it and history is now replete with open admirers of the Gita, such as Albert Einstein, Aldous Huxley, Hermann Hesse, J Robert Oppenheimer, Albert Schweitzer, Ralph Waldo Emerson, etc. who had deliberated over the timeless message of the text.

Will Durant, many years ago, felt that in many ways, India is mother of us all. He stated: "India was the motherland of our race, and Sanskrit the mother of Europe's languages: she was the mother of our philosophy; mother, through the Arabs, of much of our mathematics; mother, through the Buddha, of the ideals embodied in Christianity; mother, through the village community, of self-government and democracy. Mother India is in many ways the mother of us all".

Second World War was over. Damage was calculated. Numbers of dead were counted. Cost of the war was determined. Effects on society were studied. It had been devastating. Never in the conscious history of man had so much loss of life and property occurred. Never before had man seen so much insanity or brutality. Humbled by the destructions left in the wake of the atomic bombs dropped on Japan, its architect, Prof. Arthur Holly Compton[7], a recipient of 1927 Physics Nobel Prize, was a much-changed man. Now at an age of 62, he found himself deeper in the philosophy of life than in the science of destruction.

When in 1954, took place the second World Religions Congress in Japan, Compton was looking for answers from among the men of wisdom. His eyes flashed with hope when, in the midst of several distinguished speakers, an ordinary looking young man from India began delivering his speech. It was about a reason-based religion and what seemed more like workable philosophy than dogmatic religious rambling. His idea was not an artificially supported and externally funded utopia or a wonderland or a Garden of Eden, but a society composed of ordinary people, with all our faults but guided by the philosophy of life as enshrined in Gita, living in a self-sustained utopian society. That Young man was Pandurang Shashtri.

---

7 Prof. Arthur Holly Compton (1892-1962), as a scientific advisor to the US government during the Second World War, headed the American OSRD, the Office of Scientific Research and Developments, that oversaw development and explosion of first nuclear bomb. It was he who had appointed J Robert Oppenheimer, an open admirer of Bhagavad Gita, as the in-charge of the code-named 'Manhattan Project' that exploded the world's first experimental nuclear bomb in the deserts of Nevada, a forerunner of the actual weapons that were dropped on Hiroshima and Nagasaki.

Pandurang Shashtri Athavale[8] painted a picture of a society based on the natural duties of man. He explained very appropriately that anything unnatural cannot work in the long run. Selfishness, greed, lust, hunger, sickness, war, ego, possessiveness are all part and parcel of human nature and that they cannot be wished away. And they cannot go away by giving or receiving sermons. They have never gone and they will never go. Any philosophy that presupposes the elimination of these human weaknesses while dealing with the establishment of a society will be unsuccessful in practice. He contended that the trick lay in sublimating these human characteristics by applying them to higher purposes and that the way to do this was the philosophy of Krishna in the Bhagavad Gita.

The verbal demonstration made Compton interested in what Pandurang Shashtri had to offer—the grandeur of Vedic times, a society of Lord Krishna's ideals in which people were instinctively charitable rather than being selfish, supportive rather than exploitative, renunciating rather than accumulating, a society where everyone spent a definite period of life on education, another on earning a livelihood, another on helping others and yet another in the contemplation of God or the Ultimate Reality. And also a society where parents were held in as high an esteem as God, not mere mortals who had

---

8 Compton needed Pandurang Shastri to join him in USA. But he did not accept Compton's generous offer. Pandurang Shastri had other plans. Compton was not the one to take no for an answer, he persisted. He approached his philosopher friend in New Delhi, Dr. Radhakrishnan, who was then the Vice-President of India. He too tried, firstly through then Governor of the erstwhile Bombay State, Mr. Harekrishna Mehtab and then himself personally. But Pandurang Shastri, on a bigger mission, his dream; setting up a center for learning philosophies, (Tatva-Jnyan Vidyapeeth, Near Mumbai) and reinforced what his father had started, the Bhagavad Gita learning centre (Bhagavad Gita Pathshala). Both are very active institutions till date working in a steady and silent manner, without any publicity or accepting any patronizing by anyone. It is a fiercely independent entity, intent of doing work that would be 'liked by God, it is immaterial if it is liked (or disliked) by people.'

succumbed to lust, where teachers and masters were given the same respect that is reserved for God; not reducing them to be just paid servants, mere employees, whose 'job' it is to teach for an agreed wage and where a guest was not a stranger or an imposter but one as worthy of respect as God. On the other hand, any society, however good, can and will always succumb to lower instincts. A ball in motion, left to it, always stops after a certain time. Even the utopia can get corrupt. Philosophy of Gita comes to help even in that circumstance. Misunderstandings, wars, diseases, deaths, calamities, draughts, floods, storms etc can and will occur. A healthy society would be prepared to face these challenges when imposed and would overcome them.

Compton was captivated by the versatility of the philosophy of Gita. He noted that this philosophy was equally useful in the times of peace and war, in health and in sickness. Compton's intellect could not reconcile other philosophies that talked about the love, peace and equality but could not stand up to realities of life. Love professing religions were loveless and peace professing religions were peaceless. He saw that the philosophy of Gita takes care of all human needs. Not needing different philosophies for different situations. He got his answer.

Huston Smith, in his famous book, The Religions of Man', while discussing about Hinduism says; "It is as if it starts with man's wants. What does a man want?" Anything and everything that we want or do not want will ultimately boil down to a single unified sum of all desires. That single desire is the desire to progress, to grow, to develop or say to evolve. Life is all about progress, growth, development and evolution. All life forms, potently or latently, want to grow; therefore, knowingly or unknowingly we all are hurtling towards growth. No one is an exception. Vedas, the holy books of knowledge, have captured this innate happening within ourselves and applied it to help take us where we want to reach. The Gita, it seems, is our tool for the journey, a handbook of life.

As true for every book, it is evermore so in case of Gita, more the intensity of the quest, more knowledge it will yield. It is, though seen as a holy book of Hindus; essentially Gita is 'non-religious' in its content. It does not anywhere describe religious practices and rituals. Mainly it exudes importance of one's duty, purity of heart and mind, self-less work, spirit, laws of reincarnation, human nature, how to overcome human limitations to eventually obtain freedom from all wants, living in equanimity etc. These things are explained with appropriate similes, elaborations and philosophies related to our very being. It is like a handbook of life (and death). In the words of Aldous Huxley, "The Bhagavad Gita is the most systematic statement of spiritual evolution of endowing value to mankind. It is one of the most clear and comprehensive summaries of perennial philosophy ever revealed; hence its enduring value is subject not only to India but to all humanity."

The Gita is a conversation, mainly between Krishna, a leader of Vrushni-Yadavs, and Prince Arjun of Kuru Dynasty, taking place on a battlefield just before the commencement of a major battle. It is in the response to Arjun's dilemma, that Krishna explains him the duties of a Kshatriya[9] prince. In doing so; he discusses a number of different philosophical ideas. Arjun, famous for his prowess at archery, was a veteran of many wars. He had undergone advanced higher education in the use of most powerful of the weaponry[10] of those times. He was not the

---

9 Commonly the word 'Kshatriya' is translated by most as 'warrior', more appropriate and the literal translation of the word however is 'protector'. Kshatriya is a class of people, who in ancient times were rulers, soldiers, state administrators etc and not merely warriors.

10 Arjun had undergone training in the weapons of mass destruction with guided missiles, known as 'Pashupatashtra'. This weaponry is said to be similar but more advanced than current atomic weapons and targeting systems. They are said to be capable of multiple heads, multiple targets and have a capability to be called back after firing or even change the course midway of the flight to another target, all at the command of the user.

one, easy to convince. Krishna had a tough task, one line reply was not good enough; Arjun needed to be totally convinced and in as short a time as possible. Arjun had many counter-questions. Krishna goes an extra mile to provide answers to all that he wanted to know, till he says with satisfaction that: "By Your grace, Lord Krishna, my delusion is destroyed, I have gained Self-knowledge, my confusion is dispelled and I shall do as You said". (18.73)

Likewise, we too get our answers to our own dilemmas in life just as millions have received over thousands of years. It remains the oldest single text to hold that distinction uninterrupted for millennia. The Gita is the guide for our own purification, progress, growth, development and evolution.

Hardly any wonder, therefore, if the Gita is translated in the highest number of languages. Indeed even Bible is translated in the same or perhaps higher number of languages; however, there is a difference. The difference lies in the fact that the Hinduism being a non-proselyting religion, it does not seek to convert people, therefore not needing the Gita to be mass-printed for propaganda and free mass-distribution on the lines of Bible or Koran. The Gita has been translated and printed by individuals or some NGOs mainly with the desire that vast storehouse of knowledge be made available to readers and help make their lives better. Hinduism has kept deliberate distance from any patronizing institutions, State-sponsored or State-controlled institutions like Vatican or Waqf that could assist printing or propagating the Gita and yet, it still gets printed, and printed in thousands. This underscorces timeless and borderless significance people attach to the Gita.

Although everyone would benefit from reading the Gita, but he will benefit more who has questions in his mind, the way Arjun had. A man who echoes the yearning of the seekers in the Vedic times: "From unreality lead me to the real, from darkness to the light, from death to immortality"; would profit more.

2

Ideas Surrounding the Bhagavad Gita—the Hinduism

Rudolf Steiner said: "In order to approach a creation as sublime as the Bhagavad Gita with full understanding it is necessary to attune our soul to it". We can light up our approach towards this extraordinary poetry by having certain clarity about the philosophic and linguistic surroundings of the Gita, so as to understand it with the spirit in which it is said. Ideas contained in Hinduism are somewhat different from those contained in other mainstream religions. A reader would soon discover how fundamentally it is different and how it was necessary to reset our mindset before jumping into the Bhagavad Gita.

How does Hinduism Work? Who is a Hindu?

Hinduism is the world's oldest living religion. It has survived for millennia despite having been subjected to brutal religious expansionism. It has no single founder, no single book, no single authority, no single holy place, no religious expansionism, no religious intolerance, and even not a single, exclusive name of God. This is something unknown to most people. And Hindus, who make up about 13 percent of the world's population (about a billion plus), however, are proudly conscious of this fact and do not seek to change it. Hinduism has inculcated fierce independence of mind, and its followers have not to enslave themselves to any religious body, person or philosophy, but be only led by their own experience and convictions.

With so much of autonomy, how does then Hinduism work? It looks impossible that this type of open-ended religion can work. How has it survived thousands of years? Especially the last two thousand years under the forces of cruel and deceitful religious expansionists from overseas?

Words 'Hindu' and 'Hinduism' Originated in Middle-East

The names 'Hindu' and 'Hinduism' are attached to the people from where the Bhagavad Gita originated. The unassuming people from the land of the Gita have never even named themselves as Hindu. It was a term coined by Arabs, Turks and Persians living far west of River Indus to identify their neighbours living around and to the east of River Indus. The name Indus is an Arabised and anglicized form of the original name 'Sindhu'. Name 'Sindhu' has been used for this river by Indians from the time immemorial and it still continues even now. Thus, in a distant past, the people living in India came to be known by the name Hindus by the foreigners. In Arabic and some other languages, India is 'Hind' and its residents 'Hindus.'

It is quite baffling, how the name of the people of the geographic-region became the name of their religion. With the same rationale, French would be religion of France and American would be the religion of people of America. Absurd, but that is what is the story of the word 'Hindu'. Especially after foreign invasions on India, when they were addressed as such, that this title given by the invaders got itself attached to the subjugated population. Over the centuries, it would seem that the people of the land of the Bhagavad Gita accepted the name 'Hindu' bestowed upon them by the foreigners, however, there is a tendency nowadays to refer to Hinduism by a name which is more appropriate for it, namely the 'Sanatan[11] Dharma'. A thoughtful reader will understand and correlate 'Hindu' as 'Sanatan' and 'Hinduism' as 'Sanatan Dharma'.

---

11 Translated, 'Sanatan' means: 'timeless', 'Eternal', 'that what was, is and will remain true forever', 'Older than the oldest and newer than the newest'

Mahatma Gandhi had described himself as a follower of 'the Sanatani Hindu Religion' in his article in the June issue of Young India. He wrote: 'I call myself a Sanatani Hindu, because I believe in the Vedas, the Upanishads, the Purans, and all that goes by the name of Hindu scripture, and therefore in Avatars[12] and Rebirth."

The story is not dissimilar for the name of the Indian nation; known previously by its original name as Bha(a)rat, and known now as India[13], a derivative of the word Indus. King Bharat was a great ancestor of Arjun; from whose name the country is called Bharat (Pronounced Bhaarat). The Bhagavad Gita is part of the huge work called as the Mahabharat (pronounced Mahaabhaarat), "History of Greater Bha(a)rat".

Although imposed by foreigners, the name 'India' is accepted and even after Independence, the sovereign Indian Government has continued using the name India albeit adding the name Bharat in its official naming of the country. The official name now states in its Constitution: "India that is Bharat".

The Gita belongs to that period of ancient India, when it was an intellectually progressive and materially prosperous land. It was a long time before the arrival of hordes of ruthless, insensitive, marauding invaders, who wanted to rob the wealth of the region, take slaves, subjugate the land and serve their appetite for profane lifestyles. India has been ravaged by

12 'Avatar' is same as reincarnation in the noun form, it means, the reincarnated being. Generally applied to the God incarnate.

13 The ancient India was a large territory. By some estimates, it covered territory from Iraq to Thailand, from Southern-Tibet to Sri Lanka and from Afghanistan to Indonesia. This part of the world was known in the ancient times variously as 'Aryavarta', 'Jambu Dwip', 'Bharaat Khand' etc. The political structure was very elitist, that of a loose-confederation with many independent kings, all sovereign yet following dictates of Manu specified for the king, the 'Raj-Dharma' (Manu's code of King's Duties).

savages for millennia, and its people have lived under brutal conditions; massacred, heavily taxed, forbidden to follow their own religion, forcefully or craftily converted to foreign faiths. Divested of a learned Hindu leadership, during the age of subjugation, India gradually fell into darkness of ignorance, depravation and social ills. Fortunately, most of these evils are recognized by Hindu society and their leaders are neither hiding nor defending them, true to the tenets of Hinduism, and are actively engaged in spreading awareness and reformation.

The Hindu view of reformation is very different from that of other religions. Hinduism views reformation as a continuous process, and therefore it does not find it self-shackled by any 'isms', dogmas, books or persons, however, weighty and respected they may be; the Gita and the Lord Krishna included.

Many thoughtful individuals have tried to define Hinduism, but have failed to describe it fully. However, one can use that which has been the conclusion of the bench of learned judges of Indian Supreme Court who, taking every help from many past and present philosophers, before arriving at their conclusion tried their bit (while considering a case related to Ramakrishna Mission in August, 1995):

"When we think of the Hindu religion, we find it difficult, if not impossible, to define Hindu religion or even adequately describe it. Unlike other religions in the world, the Hindu religion does not claim any one prophet; it does not worship any one God; it does not subscribe to any one dogma; it does not believe in any one philosophic concept; it does not follow any one set of religious rites or performances; in fact, it does not appear to satisfy the narrow traditional features of any religion or creed. Confronted by this difficulty, Dr. Radhakrishnan realized that; to many, Hinduism seems to be a name without any content. Is it a museum of beliefs, a medley or rites, or a mere map, a geographical expression? [*The Hindu View of Life* by Dr. Radhakrishnan]. Having posed these questions which disturbed foreigners when they think of Hinduism, Dr. Radhakrishnan has explained how Hinduism has steadily absorbed the customs and ideas of people with whom it has come into contact and has thus been able to maintain its supremacy and its youth. Lokmanya Bal Gangadhar Tilak, in his Gitarahasya has described Hinduism as "Acceptance of the Vedas with reverence; recognition of the fact that the means or ways to salvation are diverse; and the realization of the truth that the number of gods to be worshipped is large, that indeed is the distinguishing feature of Hindu religion".

Hinduism believes and who doesn't, that life is all about living and better living? But they go beyond conventional better living. Every one, be it a new born child or be him an ailing man on his death-bed, they all 'work' and 'experience' every single moment. No one can stop 'experiencing'. Experience lets the worker modify, alter and evolve. People improve after making mistakes; some may improve early and some late but one eventually will. Death is never an end or even an obstacle. Life is a step on a road towards the goal. Hinduism in one sentence is nothing other than walking the path towards self-improvement. It is most important to be purer in mind and in action. It is more important to be good rather than look good. It does not matter what God one prays to or how many times you pray, but it is the purity of mind and action that alone matters.

He is a Hindu, who accepts all, who is sensitive to all, who is concerned only with doing his duties in the best possible way and who wants to evolve at every moment, materially and spiritually. A traditional Hindu generally accepts continuity of life (rebirth), and respects everyone. His method of worship can be different and sometimes confusing to others, however still making complete sense to that worshipper.

Nothing is Blasphemous, None is Heretic, Apostate or Murtadd

In Hinduism, no one can be blasphemous and no one can be a heretic. None can be punished for holding views, religious or irreligious. In this respect, Hinduism is much unlike the other religions of the world. Priestly authority over life, death and thoughts of the adherents is minimal. Hindu priests and holy men are not empowered to judge or punish people on account of their beliefs, their speech or their actions. Hence 'fatawas', 'cherems' and 'excommunications' do not exist in Hinduism. The scriptures have recommended only two duties for Hindu priests and holy men: to learn and to teach, life long.

Romain Rolland (1866-1944), the French Nobel laureate, and great thinker, said of Hinduism: "Religious faith in the case of the Hindus has never been allowed to run counter to scientific laws, moreover the former is never made a condition for the knowledge they teach."

Over the ages there have been so many learned men and women from among the Abrahamic[14] religions, who have suffered because their acts and beliefs were termed blasphemous or heretical.

Nicholas Copernicus (1473-1543) was the first modern astronomer to advance idea of heliocentrism as opposed to the prevalent church's position of Geocentrism. So afraid was Copernicus that he did not even discuss this subject until he became old, and his book On the Revolution of the Celestial Spheres was published only after his death, that too in Latin, so that only a few can understand it, minimizing any possible Church reaction. Despite all these precautions, after 73 years of its publication, Church did discover the book in 1616 and placed it on its Index of Prohibited Books.

---

14 Abrahamic faiths are those originated from Abraham—Judaism, Christianity and Islam.

During the Renaissance, Martin Luther (1483-1546), who was himself a monk, well educated in university and in many ways a 'more religious Christian than Pope', the founder of Protestantism, was excommunicated by Pope Leo X on January 3, 1521 for holding views different from those held by the then Catholic Church.

Giordano Bruno (1548-1600), although an ordained priest, was tried by Church for seven years for holding opinions contrary to the religion, speaking against it and its ministers, for believing in reincarnation and denying of Mary's virginity. He was pronounced guilty; his conviction was agreed even by Pope Clement VIII. He was brought to the market square with his tongue in a gag; he was tied to a pole naked and burnt alive at the stake, on February 17, 1600.

A Jew, Baruch Spinoza (1632-1677), a philosopher who thought God as Nature, was excommunicated from his Jewish faith for holding a variant opinion on the nature of God. For the apostasy he was issued strict 'Cherem' and expelled from the faith. Fearing reprisals, he could not publish his many works. Some of his important works such as The Ethics had to be published only after his death.

The life-story of Galileo Galilee (1564-1642), a devout Italian Catholic, is well known. He was a teacher at a university, and an accomplished astronomer. In spite of it, he was forced to recant his heliocentric idea that with the sun in centre, the earth revolves around it. In 1614, from the pulpit Father Tommaso Caccini (1574–1648) denounced Galileo. He was ordered to stand trial on suspicion of heresy in 1633 and was sentenced. He was required to reject heliocentrism and ordered to be jailed; the sentence was later commuted to house arrest, his dialogue forbidden and was banned from publishing any work in future. Pope Urban VIII believed: "The proposition that the sun is in the center of the world and immovable from its place is absurd, philosophically false, and formally heretical;

because it is expressly contrary to Holy Scriptures". Despite many representations, stubbornly the Pope resisted all efforts to have Galileo pardoned.

Johannes Kepler (1571-1630), the German mathematician and astronomer, was a very religious man who had originally planned to be a priest of the Lutheran Church. He discovered what is known today as 'Kepler's Laws' defining elliptical orbits of planets and many other things. Because he was Lutheran, he was persecuted by Catholic German Empire and because he did not agree in toto with Lutheran Church, he was denied even Sacrament there. Harassed by both, he was forced to constantly relocate from place to place.

Even the Legendary Joan of Arc, became victim of Church. She was tried for sorcery and heresy, and burned at the stake.

Inquisition, the most feared tool of the Church, lasted for centuries in Europe, and in Spain it lasted even longer, 354 years, notwithstanding modern-day developments! It wasn't deactivated until 1834, when the Queen Mother Cristina at last announced its repulsion: "It is declared that the Tribunal of the Inquisition is definitely suppressed." The last recorded death attributed to Spanish Inquisition occurred as late as in 1826 when a poor schoolmaster, Cayetano Ripoll was garroted to death.

Mansour Ibn Hallaj (857-922), was a Sufist, killed in Baghdad by Abbasid Caliph and Vizir Hamd because he preached a synthesized religion by taking elements that were already present in that geographical area; from Zoroastrianism-Mazdaist, Buddhist-Hindu, Shamanist, and Shia Islam. He thought that the purpose of the religious rites was to purify one's heart and it was attainable without having to follow Sunni or Shia forms of worship.

Ibn Rushd (1126-1198), also known in Europe by the name Averroes, was a medical doctor, philosopher, lawyer, logician and astronomer all rolled in one. He translated Aristotle's work, and was pioneer in thinking about separation of religion from politics. He thought that all humans are basically one at the level of soul. He advocated need for the analytical mind for interpreting Koran. His abilities were recognised and he held high positions with government of the day. Notwithstanding these, this brilliant man was condemned for heresy and spent his last days excommunicated in Morocco. Also, his religious writings were burnt.

Ibn Sina (980-1037), known as Avicenna in Europe, is regarded very respectfully as 'father of modern medicine'. He was a child prodigy and had memorized Koran when he was just seven years old. He is hailed as an accomplished mathematician. He was one of the most prominent scholars of Muslim world. Even he was suspected of infidelity. His opinion on resurrection, qadim, etc were challenged by orthodox Muslims and considered him a 'Kafir'. To avoid confrontation, Ibn Sina had to accept that what he believed was perhaps not correct. Even after his death the accusations of heresy, free thought and atheism were repeatedly leveled against him.

Zakariya Ar Razi (865-925), born near Tehran, is said to be one of the best Islamic philosophers, a medical doctor, a voracious writer having written more than 200 books on a variety of subjects. He was publicly condemned for blasphemy and all his works on religion were destroyed.

Yahya A Suhaawardi (1155-1191), founder of 'School of Illumination', was Sufist and was executed in Syria for apostasy.

Skeptic Persian poets such as legendary Ommar Al Khayyam (1048-1131) and Hafiz (1320-1389), considered to be among the world's leading poets, had to several times explain their writings, camouflage it to mean something else (double meaning) or hide them. Shaykh Ibn Al Arabi's work was banned.

In today's times, we know that the works of Salman Rushdie, the award winning British author, of Indian origin, Bangladeshi authoress Taslima Nasrin and several others are banned and they are living under constant fear of death authorized by their own religious leaders through Fatawas. Thousands of other lesser known men and women are humiliated, jailed, tortured and killed for being brave enough to hold on to their opinions which were not in line with official positions of their religious establishments.

But Hinduism gives full freedom to its followers to follow, to partially follow, to just quit following, to join any other religion, to oppose Hinduism and after all these, it even allows return anytime to Hinduism at their own wish, without any formality. This is in stark contrast to the practice followed by the other dominant faiths of the world. Islam prescribes death for the Murtadd (apostate). Murtadd is a Muslim who converts to another religion and is, therefore, someone whose blood may be freely shed. The fear of being branded 'heretic' or an 'infidel' kept many Muslim scholars away from research, from exploring religion and science beyond a certain limit and certainly the world is poorer without their contributions and not to mention the terrible loss inflicted on mankind when they have destroyed the works of the gifted minds.

Romain Rolland said in one of his essays: "The true Vedantic spirit does not start out with a system of preconceived ideas. It possesses absolute liberty and unrivalled courage among religions with regard to the facts to be observed and the diverse hypotheses it has laid down for their coordination. Never having been hampered by a priestly order, each man has been entirely free to search wherever he pleased for the spiritual explanation of the spectacle of the universe."

Idol-Worship

Idolater, heathen and, pagan, are the words used contemptuously to describe followers of non-Semitic faiths.

Followers of Semitic[15] faiths look down upon idols. They probably saw a degenerated form of Idol worship in the Arabian Peninsula and hence guided by early dictates, they threw the baby with the bath-tub, negating major benefits of scientific-idol-worship that could have otherwise accrued to their society.

Hindus understand both, accept both and appreciate both; the idol-worship[16] and the idol-less worship.[17] Both are valid and have merits of their own and therefore Hinduism has kept both options open to its followers. Mahatama Gandhi and Rabindra Nath Tagore, both Hindus and both great men, but one held idol worship as important while the other, the idol-less. They were once engaged in a conversation related to idols. Rev. C F Andrews, who was very close to Mahatma Gandhi, was present during the discussion. He has noted their arguments. In his diary, Andrews notes: "Gandhi defended them (idol-worship), believing the masses incapable of raising themselves immediately to abstract ideas. Tagore cannot bear to see the people eternally treated as child. Gandhi quoted the great things achieved in Europe by the flag as an idol; Tagore found it easy to object, but Gandhi held his ground, contrasting European flags bearing eagles etc, with his own, on which he has put a spinning wheel". Mahatma Gandhi demonstrated the concept of idol and its tremendous value.

15 Semitic religions are: Judaism, Christianity and Islam.

16 Idol-worship is known in Indian languages as 'Murti-Pooja'. Idol worship can be described as 'worshipping God having 'form and qualities'' also it can be described as 'worshipping personal God'

17 A lot of analytical study has been made by Hindus on the subject of Idol-less-worship. It is further split in two parts. 'Worshipping a formless and attribute less God' and 'worshipping a formless yet a God with attributes'. Some philosophers attribute God to have no form and no attributes (qualities) while some accept that though the God is formless, He has attributes (qualities). These two distinctions are known in the Indian languages as 'Nirgun-Niraakar-Pooja' and 'Niraakar-Sagun-Pooja' respectively. Together, both types of Idol-less worship are also known as 'worshipping impersonal God'.

Idol-less worshippers in Hinduism date back thousands of years before the advent of Abrahamic faiths, and therefore it is not a new concept for Hindus. Its clear reference and implications are found in the Gita. Lord Krishna approvingly of idol-less-worship says at 12-3 and 12-4: "Those who worship the unchangeable, the inexplicable, the invisible, the omnipresent, the inconceivable, the unchanging, the immovable, and the formless impersonal aspect of God; restraining all the senses, even-minded under all circumstances, engaged in the welfare of all creatures, also attain Me (God)." In recent times, the great Hindu reformer, Swami Dayanand Saraswati (1824-1883), re-propagated idol-less worship and even established an organization known as 'Arya Samaj' for propagating it. This organization had early successes and even now remains an influential organization. The followers of Arya Samaj meditate without any idol. Thus, in a sense Abrahamic faiths have followed the ancient idol-less-worship of Hindus.

Also, on the other hand, millions of other followers of Hinduism meditate on one or more of the many idols, pictures of 'God', 'Murti' (a statue, in which has been invoked the essence or spirit of that deity whose shape the statue conforms) to or symbols. Recommending the idol worship, Lord Krishna, sums up for us at 12-5 and 12-6 that the idol-less worship is fine but is fraught with difficulties. In His own words: "Self-realization is more difficult for those who fix their mind on the impersonal, unmanifest, and formless Absolute; because, comprehension of the unmanifest by embodied beings is attained with difficulty. For those who worship the Supreme with unswerving devotion as a personal deity of their choice, offer all actions to Me, intent on Me as the Supreme, and meditate on Me; I swiftly become their saviour from the world that is the ocean of death and transmigration whose thoughts are set on My personal form, O, Arjun."

Properly understood, the idol-worship could be a tool for self-development, the most powerful tool that uses our own psychological engine to propel us on the highway of evolution and deliver divinity into us. Pandurang Shashtri Athavale has described scientific-idol-worship as the 'greatest gift the Hindus have given to the mankind'. Christians do not generally accept idol worship, however they have accepted the benefit of worship using the icons from early era of Christianity; famously the icon of St. Nicholas of Tussa in use from approx: 245 AD. The cross itself is the most important Christian icon, kept omnipresent at their religious centres. In the later times Cardinal Nicholas of Cusa (1401-1464 AD) also used symbols and images.

Scientific-Idol-Worship

It is the most common argument of the idol worshippers that the idol is a helpful tool for concentration. They say that one's mind can easily focus on a physical form instead of an abstract idea of God. Thus they classify idol as a tool for concentration or meditation. True, but it is underselling a more glorious concept.

Even idol-less worshippers do achieve concentration, instead of any idol, using their own breathing rhythm, they meditate by focusing on inhalation and exhalation. Thus, concentration or meditation can be done by anyone, with or without an idol. The resultant sense of peace and tranquility is accrued in both the methods.

Hinduism goes beyond feeling the sense of tranquility and peace. The added value of meditation using an idol lies in its ability of providing a means of evolution and self-development. In Hinduism, God is not merely for asking mercy and blessings but every Hindu process must focus on introspection and thereby self-development and evolution; it must be a self-transformative tool.

What is the meaning of worship but to appreciate? Worshipper is appreciator of divine. For the purpose of self-development, a worshipper is expected to meditate on the idol of his choice and remember the personality of that idol during meditation. If the qualities represented in the idol are to the worshipper's liking, they begin to get absorbed and get imbibed into the worshipper, slowly but certainly and even without his knowledge, due to auto suggestion and the mind's ability to adopt. Idol worship harnesses own innate strength of mind and puts to use in self-development. Negating idol-worship negates an important benefit of God-given natural mental ability.

Hinduism gives freehand in choosing one's idol based on his own nature and one's own ambition. Idol can be an image of Jesus or Lord Rama or Lord Shiv. It can be any one. Knowingly or unknowingly we, all, each of us, are idol-worshippers. For a small child, its father or mother is an idol. For some of us, idol may be teacher or a leader or a sportsman. 'You become what you appreciate'. You are what you think. A person contemplating on Jesus tends to become like Jesus. Contemplation of brave imbibes bravery and that of cruel imbibes cruelty. Woman contemplating on men makes her a manly-woman and a man becomes womanly-man thinking of women. Their likes-dislikes and other changeable aspects would undergo changes. We are told that after filming 'Mahatma Gandhi' the actor Ben Kingsley was so touched by the character he played that before he realized, his life and views had changed, more in line with that of the Mahatama. Idol worship leads to self-discovery and consequent self-development. This is the power of idol worship, the self-development. It would indeed be naive to expect that God will emerge out of the idol. Hindus do not think of 'God in the idol' in that sense.

Having invoked the divinity in the idol, Hindu, when worshipping it, worships the essence of that presumed shape that the idol represents. It is not anymore the statue of Lord Krishna but it is Lord Krishna Himself to whom he worships paying full respect as if Lord Krishna is physically there. Major difference between the Christian icon and the Hindu idol is that while the Christian icon represents a symbol of divinity, the Hindu idol is considered by its devotee as divinity itself once the idol is sanctified by rituals, invoking the divinity in that idol.

Divinity in the idol is in the worshipper's mind. He worships with clarity that the God is physically in front of him. It is for him to assume this to obtain maximum mileage. The God seen in the idol by the worshipper is his private and personal imagery. It is for him alone and meant for providing help and inspiration for his evolution. He is therefore undaunted by the criticism from those who might ridicule him for assuming God in the image. Those who ridicule are perhaps exhibiting arrogance and incomplete-knowledge when they presume that they know it well that God cannot assume a particular form. Think for a moment, why not? Is God incapable of choosing a form for Himself if He wants to? Surely the God that can make all the forms in the universe can take a form for Himself, if He chooses to. It is our arrogance to presume on His behalf.

Over and above the 'quality-transfer' facilitated by it, the idol-worship has one more powerful dimension. It automatically creates a 'relationship' between the idol and the worshipper; his relationship with the God. Many religions of the world invoke God as 'Father'. In Israel, God is called Father. Among Christians, the trinity that God is, is the 'Father, Son and the Holy Spirit'. God is father, we are His children. God is creator and we are creatures. Hindus are allowed a bigger spectrum of relationships in Hinduism. Personification of God is the unique brilliance of Hinduism. A Hindu can consider God as Father, for some God is a mother. In the same way, God can be worshipped as a brother, as a sister, as a son, as a husband, as a lover, as a teacher or as any other relationship by a Hindu. He worships the Lord not only with that love but even the responsibility that comes with relationship that he chooses. A woman, who worships God as her small child, will never demand anything from Him, the way a mortal mother provides but never demand anything from the child. A woman, who worships God as her husband, gives up her entire self in His service, faithful to Him and Him alone. A person, who considers God as father, will do everything to be a worthy son and make Him proud, thereby purifying his conduct to become a righteous man. Ramakrishna Paramhans worshipped God as mother, Mira Bai worshipped God as her husband and women of Gokul worshipped God as their lover. That the God transcends the human relationships and even the distinction between sexes; that He is neither a son, nor a lover and nor a husband, that He is neither man nor woman, is well understood by Hindus. However, the 'relationship' becomes a tool of development. Relationship of father-child, mother-child, husband-wife, etc. draws upon human experience and helps devotee realize God's vicinity and his love in a much powerful manner. Love is a divine quality. Different relationships have love with different flavors, but all forms of love are divine. Love of father-child, of mother-child, of husband-wife, of teacher-student, of brother-sister, of friends, etc has different flavors and different aspects. Worshipping an idol creates a relationship with God and, in the process, these worshippers evolve to be able to live up to that relationship with God. This relationship concept adds value to the idol worship of Hindus and makes God 'personal' to him.

Idol worship lends triple advantages; helps in concentration and meditation, helps in self-development and helps in creating personal relationship with God; altogether helping an individual to evolve to be a better human by inculcating divine attributes that he has associated with the idol.

Worshipping Tree-God, Monkey-God, River-God and More

Worshipping is a way of saying thanks to the God and of appreciating contribution He has made to our lives. A Hindu wants to acknowledge that he, a human, is not the controller or owner of the world, but a small element, endowed with intellect enough to understand and refrain from becoming an arrogant exploiter of the resources, that are collective asset of the whole mankind. Even a stone has life within; do not the electrons move in it without any human contraption? Hindus did not need Neil Bohr (1885-1962) to tell that atom has energy within it. Neither did Hindus wait for 'matter and wave theory' to understand that the matter is wave and wave is matter, inter-convertible; simplified as energy, dynamic or potential; was already known to the ancient Indian philosophers. It is well known that Sage Kanaad,[18] the ancient Indian atomic scientist, had shown his preparedness to even worship atomic particles.

For a Hindu, everything is divine and he is proud to worship all life and so-called 'life-less' forms. They worship the mountains, rivers and seas. They worship flower, fruits, plants and trees, they worship animals and birds. Himalayas and its various peaks are revered. Vindhya and Girnar mountains are revered. They undertake hazardous treks to Mount Kailash, and Mount Kedar seated deep in the Himalayas. They walk to the sources of the rivers Ganges, Yamuna, Brahmaputra, Indus, Narmada, etc braving awfully tough climb and spending their lives' saving on it. They say that a dip in Ganges will cleanse one's sins, if done with right spirit and resolve not to repeat. They worship ocean before setting out to fish. They worship Sun, Moon and all the planets. They worship Banayan tree, Peepal tree, Neem tree, Tulsi (Basil) plant, the lotus flower, coconut fruit, betel nut, Rudraksha seed and several others including the deadly poisonous dhatura plant. The list includes peacock,

18 Kanaad name was given to the sage due to his obsession with atomic particles. Kan is a simplified word for atom and the Kanaad stands for still smaller parts of the atom. He was an atheist, who saw the origin of universe in an atom rather than in God.

crow, swan, eagle, mouse, tiger, lion, bull, cow, turtle and many more. As practising worshippers, Hindu fishermen refrain from fishing during June-July-August period, said to be the breeding period of marine creatures, thus letting sea rejuvenate itself. They refrain from plucking from trees and plants at night, when they are thought to be 'sleeping'. They never kill animals for sport[19]. They never kill a cow or a bull. Many practising worshippers will eat meal only after first feeding pigeons, dogs, cows, fish and even ants. In rural India even today, in many households the first two 'Roties' ('Roti' is Indian flat Bread) are cooked every day for cows and dogs and only thereafter they are cooked for the family. Hindu calendar is also very special in the sense that it brings man closer to the nature unlike any other calendar currently in wide scale use.

Even the soil is precious. The land of India is considered as most sacred. They have personified India as Goddess-Mother-India. Perhaps the country is chunk of soil, dust and stones for some politicians; it is a deity with her picture adorning many homes. There are hymns[20] in her name and people swear to lay down their lives serving her. When India was divided in two parts by the British, Hindus were traumatized not only because of forced migration and loss of the territory but also because they could not bear the severing of their Goddess,the Mother India.

There are designated Gods or Devas, who personify various elements that are around us, such as Water, Air, Mountains, Rivers, Oceans, Animals, Trees, Plants, Flowers, Fruits, etc. Everything is sacred and should be protected, used only when compelled, and only in the minimum quantity. Hindus consider the entire earth as holy and is personified as Earth-Goddess making it all sacred and worthy of worship and

---

19 Killing for sport is forbidden in Hindusim. An exception is made for the Royals, so that they can practice their archery skills.

20 'Vande-Mataram' written by Bankim Chandra Chattopadhyay is the most famous hymn, saluting the nation, singing which thousands of freedom fighters laid down their lives fighting colonial rulers and won their freedom.

thereby taken care of. Stars, planets and constellations too are sacred, making them subjects of deeper study as demonstrated by perhaps the world's only stellar[21] calendar. A date specified in the Hindu calendar is very expressive. Given a date, it provides precise position of Sun, (therefore season), the phase of Moon, and location of all 12 constellations. Therefore, Hindu calendar is known as a stellar instead of usual solar or lunar calendars. Hindus celebrate festivals associated with seasons, phases of moon and movements of sun.There are thousands of temples where the stars and planets are personified as deities and worshipped.

Anyone who has had a brush with Findhorn foundation[22], as known what results were achieved by the founders Peter and Eileen Caddy after they prayed to 'plants spirits', addressing them as the "Deva", Sanskrit word for Demi-Gods. They grew huge vegetables and fruits by praying to 'Cabbage-Deva', 'Pea-Deva', 'Tomato-Deva' etc. 40-pound cabbage that they produced became a legend, grown on a piece of cold-windy land where nothing could grow. They even prayed to the crop-destroying insects requesting them to move away; and the pests did move away from their farm! But it is no surprise, ancient Hindu sages, who moved and lived all-alone in the forests infested with wild animals, did not need any weapons to keep wild beasts away. Hindus believe that everything has life. Stated differently, divinity resides into everything; and

---

21 Stellar Hindu calendar is mistakenly identified as Lunar calendar. Islamic calendar is lunar calendar and in it, the connection between the season and the month is lost. The Gregorian calendar suffers from the fact that its dates do not reveal the phases of moon. And none of these two show any connection with the constellations. As the Hindu calendar connects all the three elements, it is known as stellar calendar.

22 Findhorn Foundation was established in 1962 in Scotland by Peter Caddy, Eileen Caddy and Dorothy MacLean. It is a thriving community with several ecologically sustainable eco-villages and spiritual centres. For more details, check their website: www.findhorn.org

one can connect to these things as demonstrated by Peter and Eileen Caddy.

Some faiths have split the God's creation in two parts. 'Man' and 'Things' and they have somehow assumed that man has been 'granted' ownership and power over 'things'. 'Things' are animals, plants and all the rest that is found around man. Most of us, we humans, arrogate that we are 'supreme' and that everything else as subservient to us. By removing the sense of divinity in 'things', those have led the world into naked exploitation of resources, extinction of spieces and irreversible environment disaster; the very things that were to be prevented by the faiths. For Hindus, there is no such division. Man should humbly look after and support everything, humans, animals, plant, water, stone, soil, air or space. By Pranayam, they even regulate intake of air. The idea is to use all the resources in an efficient manner; even the free-resource that air is, in an efficient way, a way in which the resource gives maximum impact with a minimum intake; just enough to survive whereby the world remains our habitat for longest possible time.

A Hindu worships and thus respects cow, bull, elephant, serpent, cobra, eagle, peacock, swan, turtle, mouse, and host of other creatures who have been given a place of pride in the society by designating a special deity with whom they would also be respected. Goddess Lakshmi goes with elephant, Lord Shiv goes on bull and Lord Ganesh travels on mouse, dog goes with Lord Dattatreya and so on.

All these acts of Hindus keep the God and His creation, in their active consciousness, bringing them closer to nature in every activity from morning till night thereby letting them become more sensitive, modest and charitable. In other words, this worship leads one to the self-development with healthy development of society and the environment.

Do Hindus worship monkeys, snakes and trees? Yes, emphatically they do; and why not, if it helps the whole world, its inhabitants and simultaneously benefits self-evolution into a sensitive and considerate individual?

One God or Many Gods?

Hindus do worship many 'Gods', but it is equally true that Hindus worship only one single God. Obvious paradox! A typical logical person is entitled to ask: 'friend, please tell me straight, one God or many Gods?'

Recently, American media witnessed a lively debate on this issue. On 12 July 2007, history was made when for the first time the Senate was opened with the invocation of Hindu holy verses, at the invitation of Senate Majority Leader Harry Reid, a Democrat member from Nevada. It ran: "Let us pray. We meditate on the transcendental glory of the Deity Supreme, who is inside the heart of the Earth, inside the life of the sky, and inside the soul of the heaven. May He stimulate and illuminate our minds. Lead us from the unreal to the real, from darkness to light, and from death to immortality. May we be protected together, may we be nourished together. May we work together with great vigor. May our study be enlightening."

Without hearing the prayer, the protestors (a family, father-mother-daughter belonging to a conservative Christian anti-abortion group) branded the Hindu prayer as "a prayer of the wicked"; that it is an "abomination" and "there can be no Lord but Jesus Christ". The Senate security officers quickly removed the demonstrators, however, the next day a debate ensued in the media, suggesting me that a lot of lack of awareness existed among people on this issue; one God or many Gods? Summing up readers' views it seemed to say: "In Hinduism, you have not one God, but many, many, many, many, many gods, when they talked about Creator—that's not one that fits here because we don't know which creator we're talking about within the Hindu religion. It is time for America to wake up. Hinduism is a false religion with false gods and we have to let people know that

Jesus is the only way and the truth and the life as it says in John 14:6. Hinduism is not the way to get to heaven, only knowing Jesus and following him will enable us to get to heaven."

Gita explains eloquently in 7-21, 22; "Whosoever desires to worship whatever deity—using any name, form, and method—with faith, I make their faith steady in that very deity. Endowed with steady faith they worship that deity, and obtain their wishes through that deity. Those wishes are, indeed, granted only by Me." (The One God). Ralph Waldo Emerson had said many decades ago: "The Bhagavad Gita is an empire of thought and in its philosophical teachings Krishna has all the attributes of the full-fledged monotheistic deity and at the same time the attributes of the Upanishadic absolute."

Media reported among other things, that: 'had the protestors waited to hear the prayer in full, they would probably not behave the way they did. The prayer was in line with usual Hindu spirit of an all-inclusive God, for every one, a universal prayer meant for entire world'. Even Senator Reid defended the prayer when he took the floor, and thanking the priest for opening the Senate, he spoke of a statue of Mahatma Gandhi he keeps in his office, and added: "If people have any misunderstanding about Indians and Hindus, all they have to do is to think of Gandhi, a man who gave his life for peace. I think it speaks well of our country (USA) that someone representing the faith of about a billion people comes here and can speak in communication with our heavenly Father regarding peace".

Ancient Hindu scriptures talk about 330 million Gods. Perhaps the figure stood for the population of the planet at one time or an indication that every individual on the planet is divine. Hindus are told: 'Just as water falling from sky always leads to the Ocean, Prayer offered to any and every God, leads ultimately to 'Keshav' the One God and that "As different rivers and streams, having their sources in different places, all mingle their waters in the sea, so, O Lord, the different paths which men take through different tendencies, various though they appear, curving or straight, all lead to Thee."

Humans, animals, plants, trees, mountains, rivers, sea, planets and stars, whatever one can think of have element of divinity on account of having been created by divine. This is how a Hindu looks at it. Thus, for Hindus, many 'Gods' is a truth, and yet all these narrow down to the trinity of Creator-Sustainer-Destroyer, the Brahma-Vishnu-Mahesh is also a truth and when this trinity ultimately merges as Brahman or Paramatma, the one God is also the truth. He knows with conviction that the God that he is praying to will take him to the salvation.

Besides there being one God, when a Hindu prays to the Shiv-Ling, he understands what it signifies. The Ling stands for One and its round base stands for Zero; there is nothing in the world besides the God; God is only one and rest of all without Him is a big naught.

Infidels, Unbelievers, Heathens, Pagans and Kafirs

These have become religious swear words. 'Infidel', 'unbeliever', 'pagan', 'heathen and 'kafir' are the terms always used in a derogatory sense for the followers of non-Abrahamic faiths.

The word 'pagan' literally means 'country-dweller' (from Latin Paganus). The word 'heathen' also means the same, 'dwelling on the heath' (from Armenian "ethanos"). The practitioners of the ancient religions of Germany, Scandinavia, the Netherlands, England, and Iceland came to be called "heathens" and those in Southern Europe, became known as pagans. Till the advent of Abrahamic faiths, these words were not 'bad' words in themselves. Presumably the new religions were primarily confined to the urban areas and were yet to reach the rural, difficult to access areas, where they still continued with their traditional way of worship. However these two words, 'pagan' and 'heathen', in the vocabulary of new converts came to acquire a meaning 'polytheist' or 'not belonging to one of them' and subsequently as 'bad people' or came to be used in derision as 'those idiots'.

Infidels are the persons who are not faithful to their religion. Unbelievers and kafirs are those that do not believe in God, those who are atheists, those who have no 'book'. These words are used insultingly in the sense of crime. With these words becoming swear words, they were rampantly used to denounce anyone. Abuse of these words became so widespread even within the followers of religion that the religious leaders had to put a ban on use of these terms at least amongst 'the people of the book' (amongst Jews, Christians and Muslims). The word became the choisest term for insulting and describing followers of Hinduism and host of other ancient religions and traditions and especially pre-Christian religions.

Christianity and Islam treated heathens and pagans as idolaters; branded and persecuted as 'Satan worshippers'. Christians were taught that the pagan-folk were Satan worshippers, or simply Godless, quoting Bible: "The sacrifices of pagans are offered to demons, not to God, and I do not want you to be participants with demons."(1 Corinthians 10:20.). As a matter of fact, 'devil', 'demon' and 'satan' are invention of Abrahamic faiths; they never existed in the ancient faiths. These ancient faiths were not God-less, in fact they had many Gods, Goddesses, wights (living beings), and innumerable spirits inhabiting everything from stones to trees. Everything in the heathen cosmos is alive, and has some level of consciousness. However, misconceptions are systematically spread about them since the advent of Christianity and more since beginning of the organized Church. Pagans and heathens and those who practise the old native ethnic religions have continuously suffered insults, humiliation and physical harassment including massacres and systematic attempts to eradicate these religions from the face of the earth. In India, forest dwellers, the so-called 'adivasis' have lost their traditional values overrun by Christian missionaries in Mizoram, Jharkhand, Orissa, etc.

Quintessential to Hinduism, all of these, 'infidels', 'unbelievers', 'pagans', 'heathen and 'kafirs' are humans as anyone else. Hindus do not believe that God hates them or disowns them nor God wants to punish them. In Hinduism, none can be 'infidel'.

Tax on Dhimmi: Jizya and Kharaj

'Dhimmi' is a term that defines Christians and Jews living under Islamic rulers. Under Islamic rulers, Dhimmies were required to pay a special tax known as 'Jizya' and 'Kharaj' in return for recognizing their existence.

They had several restrictions on them, however, as an uneasy second-class citizens, they were tolerated by the rulers, being contributors of higher-tax. However, because their testimony was invalid in courts, crimes were freely committed against Dhimmies without fear of punishment, and were subject to whims of rulers and were molested by the mobs.

On the other hand, Hindu rulers always had a uniform tax structures irrespective of the religion of the subject since Hinduism does not discriminate any one on the basis of his belief. This code of conduct was never violated by Hindu kings.

Non-Dhimmis (Hindus)

Whatever 'protection' (if one can use that term) dhimmies received at the hands of Islamic rulers, was unthinkable for other non-dhimmi communities, who were without any protection whatsoever and were subjected to all types of atrocities and repression. Hindus were one of the victims falling in this category of non-dhimmies, who could not even get that 'high-priced (Jizya)' protection. (In a few odd cases, Islamic rulers of India had proclaimed, albeit very rarely, some of their subjects as 'dhimmies' enabling them to earn higher tax-money from Hindus).

Qisas, 'Eye-for-eye', Diyya, Blood-Money

If a person is murdered by someone, in Sharia law, his relatives have the right to murder (and also the right to pardon). Islam provides for religiously approved revenge (Qisas), something that is considered very demeaning among Hindus. Biblical laws also provide for 'eye-for-eye' justice; however Christians have reformed themselves over a period and have left behind that practice. As per the religion-sanctioned compensation, the murderer can pay certain compensation (Diyya or Blood-Money) to be able to escape the punishment. The amount of Diyya changed from time to time and place to place. As per the current rule in force, in Saudi Arabia, Diyya is: Riyals 100,000 for murder of a Muslim man, 50,000 Riyals for a Christian man and 6,666 for the murder of Hindu man. The compensation for murdering a woman is exactly half of man.

Among Hindus, only the judicial power has the right to punish and only the highest political authority (King or President, or Prime Minister) to pardon.

Freedom to Think, Speak and Act

Hinduism and the Bhagavad Gita abhor any authority that restricts free thinking of man. Not only that, it asks one to reject all that has been said in it if it does not conform to experienced knowledge and if it does not seem convincing.

Indeed, freedom to think, to form one's opinions and to believe in them is the cornerstone of all the ancient Indian literature. Knowledge is supreme. Teachers and students have a special place in the Indian culture. Any opinion, however outrageous it may look, can be held and be propagated without fear of a fatwa. All views are acceptable to the followers of the Gita. Men should be able to choose whatever path they feel is right for them. Light-hearted jokes about God, gods, Devas, seers, sages, saints and even about their wives exist abundantly in the Sanskrit literature; and no one raises their eye-brows. One can even argue against the Vedas, the very heart of Hinduism. A materialist called Charvak or an atheist like Kapil, are both revered and are accepted as seers by Hindus. Ancient atomic scientist-philosopher Kanaad, who believed the cause of the universe to be the atoms and not God, is also held in esteem as a seer. Hindu histories have many such sworn disbelievers but none were persecuted. This seems in great contrast to what was witnessed in Europe during the Medieval Age and throughout Islamic world till date.

Strength of allowing every shade of belief comes from a verse that says: "Truth alone prevails and not the falsehood", V-6-Mundak-2-Chp-1: "Satyameva Jayate Na Nrutam"[23] is something that Hindus have confidently believed in for thousands of years and they, therefore, do not care to persecute anyone but give them freedom and time to come to their own conclusion.

This legendary freedom of thinking is responsible for creative and unrestrained use of mental faculties. Instinctively, a Hindu accepts and respects any and every different strain of thoughts, behaviour and traditions; an important factor; a guarantee that has kept Christians, Muslims, Jews and Zoroastrians safe in India, even though Christians and Muslims came as oppressors and remained so for centuries.

Jews and Zoroastrians came to find a safe refuge and they got it from Hindus. Even today, persecuted in his own land, the Buddhist Dalai Lama is safe in India. This innate freedom in Hinduism has shaped their culture into a genuinely large-hearted welcoming people. Among other civilities, a child is taught 'the guest is to be treated as a God', "Atithi Devo Bhav".

The freedom of thinking has kept Hindu society free from entrapment faced by other societies when they faced vexing issues such as Prophet's picture, cartoons, the veil, the hijab, the circumcision male genital mutilation, the sharia, "talaq'-divorce, the polygamy, the jihad, the crusade, the honor-

23 Even in the independent India, 'Satyameva Jayate' is part of the official insignia, placed below the 4-headed Lion Symbol derived from Ashok's Pillar.

killing, the suicide-bombing, the female priests, the married church-ministers, the homosexuality, eating of pork, kosher[24], halal[25], abortion, suicide, euthanasia, gay, lesbian, etc. These issues have never become passionately debatable issues in the Hindu contexts, only because the granted freedom expresses itself in the respect for others' opinions. Being a follower of reason based religion; a Hindu does not find himself at odds when he deviates from conventional religious path to another to accommodate modernity, science, or laws of the land.

Followers of Hinduism are free to question their religious practices and their religious authorities. Nobel Prize winning Indian economist, Amartya Sen, in his book The Argumentative Indian, has given many instances of arguments and discussions that have been happening in India from time immemorial with examples dating back from Ramayan and Mahabharat. These arguments, that help provoking thoughts and reform the religion and the society, have helped Hinduism reshape it from time to time and has given space to every denomination within it.

Mankind is a Family, Unity in Diversity

The early philosophers and sages of Hinduism said: 'Vasudhaiva Kutumbakam', the whole world is one family and wished "Sarvetra Sukhina Santu, Sarve Santu Niramaya, Sarve Bhadra nu Pashyantu"; "let everyone be happy, let everyone be free from disease, and let their happiness be visible." These choicest boons are not reserved for Hindus alone but are asked for all mankind, in all the places (Sarve-everyone and Sarvetra-everywhere). Amazing broad-mindedness it is, judged from narrow perspectives that we witness around us, where directly or indirectly we exhibit our disdain for immigrants, foreigners, people of other faiths and colours.

24 Kosher is a religiously approved food specified in Judaism.

25 Halal is a religiously approved food specified in Islam.

Bhagavad Gita, 13-28 says: "When one beholds one and the same Lord existing equally in every being, one does not injure anybody; because one considers everything as one's own self. And thereupon attains the Supreme Abode."

One Power Centre: The God

In many religions and traditions of the world, they have specified two independent and rival power centers, Good and Evil or God and Satan. And that these two powers have a perpetual tug-of-war, evil triumphants more often but ultimately facing defeat from good. The concept of two power centers is not accepted in Hinduism.

'Unified Field Theory' in physics is a theory that proposes to unify four known forces by a simple set of general laws. These forces are known to control all the observed physical phenomena: 'the gravitation', 'the electromagnetism', 'the strong force' (a short-range force that holds atomic nuclei together), and 'the weak force' (responsible for slow nuclear processes as beta decay). Albert Einstein proposed this theory. He believed that all physical phenomena should ultimately be explainable by some underlying unity. This theory has fascinated the scientific community worldwide and many scientists are still working on it. It could not be proved during Einstein's lifetime. However, later in 1968, physicists Steven Weinberg and Abdus Salam had had success at identifying a common law applicable to some aspects of these four forces. Work still continues.

Like the 'Unified Field Theory', in Hinduism, Creator is one. There is only one 'power centre', the God. Everything emanates from Him. Hinduism has only God and no Satan. Everything; material, energy, animate or inanimate is God-created. Good and bad are comparative terms and they are many a times indeterminable. 'One man's meat is poison for the other'. But both, meat and poison are God created. Endowed with brilliant intelligence, a man becomes good or evil and acts accordingly. Hindus ask every human to accept his own evil tendencies and deeds and encourage them to reform, more importantly not let him pass the blame of his own misdeeds on an external agency, the Satan.

Dharma

'Dharma' means a lot of things collectively. In its accurate expression the word means 'that what upholds (society and individuals)' or as further explained, 'all those things and actions that lead to welfare of all mankind, stability of society and growth of individual'. Vaisheshika Sutra defines Dharma as: 'that from which results true happiness'. Dharma therefore means 'righteousness'.

Hinduism is more about the 'righteousness' than the 'rights'. Hindu spiritual literature rarely talks about one's rights, but focuses instead on one's duties. Duties come first; nay duty comes first, middle and last. There is hardly anything else in the essence of the Bhagavad Gita. 'Dharma' is said to be 'duty' or 'righteousness'. For instance, a student's duty is to study, a father's duty is to take care of the family, a judge's duty is to give impartial justice, a soldier's duty is to fight, a teacher's duty is to teach. A human's duty is to develop and evolve, become perfect, so perfect that one can mistake him for the 'Most Perfect', the God. The target that is almost unattainable, yet it stores so much attraction that millions are toiling for it and doing penance and austerities. If everyone abides by his own Dharma, peace, progress and prosperity will automatically follow, because when everyone is obsessed only with doing his duties towards others, overlooking everything else, who would exploit who?

Ignorants have translated the Sanskrit word 'Dharma' as 'religion'. The word 'Dharma' does not just mean 'religion'; it is religion and a lot more. It is a most interesting word with a wider meaning and stores a potential to heal the rifts between religions. Hindus, it can be said, have short-sold the word Dharma for religion leading to a lot of misunderstanding.

The word 'religion' in the English language signifies the practice of worshipping God. Its Latin root 'religio' means 'to bind together with the string of certain beliefs'. A group of people come together, share a belief system, stick together and support each other. Thus religion binds to a certain belief. In Hinduism, one has a freedom to change or accept any belief system. Hence the word 'religion' is patently inappropriate for Hinduism. And the word 'Dharma' is inappropriate for Christianity, Judaism or Islam.

The true translation of the word 'religion' happens to be the word 'Panth' (in Sanskrit and all other Indian languages). However, Buddhist started to call their way of living and beliefs by the word 'Dhamma' ('Dhamma' being a distortion of 'Dharma' by the early followers of Lord Gautam Buddha) and in a naïve innocence, when confronted with holders of different beliefs, the Muslim invaders and early Christian rangers, Hindus called their religion also as 'Dharma'. Thus what should have been a 'Muslim Panth' came to be 'Muslim Dharma' and the 'Christian Panth' became the 'Christian Dharma' in India. Thus an average Indian today thinks that Muslim, Christian, Judaism and Hinduism are all different Dharmas. By Dharma, they mean religion.

The fact is: Hinduism is a 'Dharma', the Sanatan Dharma, in addition to be a religion (its method of worship can be called as 'Hindu Panth' or 'Hindu religion'), therefore Hinduism as a whole is not comparable to any religion. Hindus should have saved the word 'Dharma' for higher causes above the religion. By equating 'Dharma' with 'religion', the grander meaning of Dharma has escaped most people who started comparing Hinduism with their religions, resulting into the petty up-manships and competitiveness, a factor in deadly humanitarian mishaps, wanton violence, venom-spewing and communal clashes, partiality and injustice.

The antidote to the religion inspired terrorism and intolerance lies singly in the concept of accepting everyone as has been demonstrated by Hinduism, not passive acceptance as 'tolerance' but active embracing everyone from the mental conviction borne out of a magnanimous open mind. It is not to prophesize, but thinkers of the world will eventually find that there simply is no other way, except learning to live harmoniously with others, said differently, to follow 'Sanatan Dharma' as done by Hindus from the time immemorial, a universal doctrine that allows multiple religious practices without hatred for other; a sane and a glorious way of coexistence. Hinduism itself has tens of thousands of sects and sub-sects with different philosophies and streams of thought, yet all live simultaneously without any bloodshed. Hindu Dharma is and should be understood by all as "Charter of Universal Human Duties", spelled as the "Sanatan Dharma". If the whole issue of Dharma was to be recharted by world's intelligents, it could be as follows: Every one calling themselves as followers of Sanatan Dharma and choosing their way of worship differently as practising Christian religion, Muslim religion, Hindu religion, Jewish religion and so on.

This kind of grouping (grouped as followers of Sanatan Dharma) will enable one to view others as part of 'his own fraternity, but merely following different customs and way of worship'. Because Santan Dharma is an inclusive 'idea' that includes all the philosophies of all the current and past religions such as Christianity, Islam, Judaism, Zoroastrianism, etc, it allows differing religious practices. Sanatan Dharma is clear in the sense that it does not say that your salvation lies only in Jesus, or only in following Ramadan Fasting, or only in repeating the name of Lord Rama, it says all these are different ways and each can help you reach the Ultimate, salvation or liberation, and conversely none of these will help you reach salvation if you are not of pure heart. Everyone could retain their individualities and yet remain one. If this grand concept of early philosopher-saints of India was properly understood, people following all the religions would have been 'People of the Sanatan Dharma' and not merely 'People of the book', idolaters, pagans, etc. It would have resulted in less bloodshed and more brotherhood.

A discerning reader will find a glaring difference in the way 'others' were, and still are, treated by Hindus over millennia and how Hindus were treated by 'others'. In the history of thousands of years can any one show even one military aggression that India may have committed on the people of other faiths? Have Hindus anytime told to anyone that his faith is wrong and therefore he should change it to Hinduism ever? Have Hindus launched any crusades ever? And yet without any aggression Hinduism still remains the religion of billion plus people today.

The Brihadaranyak Upanishad identifies Dharma with Truth. It says very eloquently: "There is nothing higher than Dharma. Even a very weak man hopes to prevail over a very strong man on the strength of Dharma, just as (he prevails over a wrong-doer) with the help of the king. So what is called Dharma is really Truth. Therefore, people say about a man who declares the truth that he is declaring Dharma and about one who declares Dharma they say he speaks the truth. These two (Dharma and truth) are this."

Why the discussion on Dharma? Because, Dharma is central to the Bhagavad Gita. Because the Pandav commander Arjun is temporarily confused about his Dharma, meaning righteousness and his duties; and Gita is the discourse to him on making him duty-bound. In our own lives, we too have a certain role, as a son, as a student, as a father, as a mother, as a brother, as a friend, as an employee, as an employer, etc. Therefore, we too have our duties. The Gita guides us into our duties, so performed that it can become 'Dharmic'; that is fruitful to us and also to others, extending stability to mankind and taking us to the ultimate 'salvation' or 'liberation', while performing our duties. Arjun is our representative and the knowledge he acquired from Lord Krishna is the knowledge that we are seeking from studies of the Bhagavad Gita.

Duties and Rights

Hindus concern themselves only with their duties, setting them apart as a people, from rest of the world following any other 'isms'. Thinking of exercising their rights does not even occur to them. This is their ethos; but perhaps not anymore. It was until the time when Vedic culture was prevalent. The language of 'rights' becomes necessary when someone is depriving the other of his 'rightful' dues. In a society where everyone was obsessed with doing their duties, the other's rights were protected by default. Every member of the society was in his 'dharma'. This was pre-Mahabharat-war-era. As per the holy Hindu scriptures, at the end of Mahabharat, 'era-of-Kali' began. Kali-era (Kali-Yug) is marked by the tendency of people wishing to deprive others of their rightful dues; be it money, help, respect or anything else.

The Hindu scriptures talk only about the 'duties' and nothing else. However, even in today's decadent period, any Hindu holy-man, if was to ask about 'rights' he would be termed as a politician or a selfish man by Hindu society. If a church priest or a mosque prayer leader was to ask for rights, a Hindu would accept that as natural but not if the similar demand is made by a Hindu religious man; he would be soon branded unreligious or opportunist by Hindus.

This is not to say that a Hindu today does not demand his rights. He does, however, most often without conviction. With gradual collapse of Vedic education, with wealth getting higher priority over knowledge, with knowledgeable accepting supremacy of the wage giving masters, with wealthy accepting subservience to the seat of political power, with entry in India of cruel plunderers, who could hardly understand indigenous culture, effectively changed an original Hindu, who then started becoming defensive, worried for his rights, though still maintaining next best attitude of 'duty first, rights then'. The killer blow to the sense of doing duties came with the advent of Marx and the Russian revolution. Now as everywhere, for a Hindu, duty, yes but only if helps. If doing duty brings trouble then, hell-with-the duty.

This is the journey from 'duty-under-any-circumstances-even-if-it-means-death' as shown in the Bhagavad Gita', to 'forget-duty,-my-rights-are-first-at-any-cost'.

Original Sin

Hinduism considers all life to be precious and sacred. The birth is sacred and so is death. Hindu does not suffer from the guilt of the 'original sin', to which the Christians are led to suffer. On the contrary, the Bhagavad Gita pronounces every individual to be intrinsically divine by the virtue of resident God in their body.

The Gita fully approves of all lawful pleasures, including what is castigated as 'sin committed' by Adam and Eve. In 7-11, Lord Krishna announces: "I am the desire, the lust that is in accord with Dharma in human beings". Therefore, the act of procreation is also sacred, albeit for righteousness or Dharma. In the Hindu 'Eden Garden', the fruit was not forbidden. In fact, in stark contrast to the Genesis story of the sin of Adam and Eve, Hindus have an interesting but opposite story of how God does not 'approve' of those who abstained and did not procreate.

Very much unlike Adam and Eve, who, in Bible, succumbed to temptation, mated and brought upon them and the mankind the burden of 'the original sin', the humans in the story of Bhagavat Puran of Hindus did not mate, did not succumb to desire. Even when implored by God, to help him populate the world, humans in the Hindu story refused to oblige, much to the chagrin of Brahma. Chief among them who was leading the group into refusal to procreate was the great renuncient sage, famously known as Narad Muni. Every time Brahma created humans, Narad would brainwash all of them into abstinence. Narad's logic was impeccable. Why to put people through endless cycle of birth and death. God, Brahma was angered by this 'non-cooperation', probably the first non-cooperation movement of humans! At one stage, as the story unfolds, Brahma becomes so enraged that he curses Narad to a life of an unending wanderer. Having thus got rid of Narad Muni, Brahma thereafter could convince the new crop of humans to begin the wheel of procreation and ensured that humans thus multiplied to populate the earth.

Narad Muni wanted to remain a celibate. Celibacy is regarded in very high esteem by Hinduism. This fact is brought home by the fact that notwithstanding anger of Lord Brahma and notwithstanding his compelling persuasion, Narad did not oblige. Celibacy or abstinence from sex is known in Sanskrit language as "Brahmacharya". Indeed Brahmacharya is a lot more beyond simply sex-abstinence. It involves indulgence in study, doing self-less work, etc, in addition to abstinence from the physical pleasures. Best known Hindu monk, Swami Vivekanand observed Brahmacharya life long, and so also thousands of others.

For a common man, Hinduism recommends a balanced life. It should have elements of all the ingredients of good life-education, sports, abstinence, enjoyment, children, trade, luxuries, self-less-service to society, peace and spiritual development. A man is not complete without all these elements. To achieve a balanced growth in every human being, Hinduism has recommended a system of 'four-Ashrams', assuming a life of 100 years, the activities are distributed thus:

1. **Brahmacharya-Ashram**: Study, abstinence from pleasures and prepare for life beyond: Up to about the age of 25 years, a Brahmachari is expected to remain a student, a celibate. At the

Gurukul (Residential schools) he is expected to wash his own clothes, make his own meal and prepare his own bed, sleep on hard surface, take shower with cold water, play vigorous games and study hard. Learning various disciplines, spiritual and moral knowledge, trade related knowledge, etc. are mandatory part of the Brahmacharya stage until his teacher confirms that the student is mature enough to go for the next Ashram.

2. **Grihastha-Ashram**: For next twenty-five years, approximately between the age of 25 and 50 years, one is required to marry, enjoy the pleasures of life, raise family, support society by business or professional activities, entertain guests, train own children to take up appropriate professions, get the children married to suitable partners when they become elligible. The 'Grihasth-Ashram' is considered the most important as the 'Grihasthi' (the house-holder) is an anchor which directly and indirectly supports rest of the three 'Ashrams'.

3. **Vanaprastha-Ashram**: Retire at the age of 50 from active work, gradually handover his duties to children and simultaneously increase time spent on society to return their obligations by guiding the needy and on God contemplation. This should be done between the age of about 50 and 75 years. This Ashram has immense potential in improving and maintaining high standards of society.

4. **Sanyas-Ashram**: Leave the house, never to return, disowning every material thing that belonged to you and spend full time in God contemplation and self-control. This is to be done after an age of 75 years. Sanyasi has no likes, dislikes, love or hate. As nothing belongs to a sanyasi and as he belongs to none, Sanyasi is held as sacred and he enjoys freedom from usual worldly conventions. Even occasional irrational behaviour is overlooked by the society respecting age and saffron robe. Saffron is the colour declaring renunciation.

Every person is unequivocally advised by the Hindu scriptures to follow the Ashrams appropriate to their age. It is considered important to marry after finishing studies and is considered to be undesirable, to be a renouncient monk before fulfilling his duty as appropriate to his Ashram-Dharma. Great sages like Swami Vivekanand or Adi Shankeracharya too had to face criticism for having jumped from 1st to 4th Ashram. Hinduism does not spare any one, spiritual rules are equal for everyone.

In the story of Narad Muni, too, he wanted straight jump to the 4th Ashram. This was not admired by Lord Brahma in the Hindu Garden of Eden.

Sin and its Antonym (Paap and Punya)

What is the antonym of the word 'sin'? English language is not a big help here. If 'sin' is a bad deed and takes you to hell. What is its antonym? A good deed that takes one to heaven? In Sanskrit, sin is 'Paap' and its antonym is 'Punya'. If sin can be taken as 'bad credit' the Punya can be approximately understood as 'good-credit'. The words, 'good' and 'bad' are utterly confusing when it comes to spirituality. On many occasions, a 'bad' looking deed is good, and is Punya. On the other hand, a 'good' looking deed is bad and earns Paap or sin. Martin Luther wanted to get married and his Church did not permit him to marry. A minister must be celibate, the Church thought. He left the Catholic Church and founded Protestantism. Catholics would consider him a sinner, doer of bad deed while the Protestants, consider him a good person.

As there is no existence of any English word that can describe 'Punya' we will use Sanskrit word as it is. To elaborate, the Punya is not merely 'righteousness' nor just 'virtue' nor only a 'good work', but it is that deed which will give you a genuine, so-called 'good credit'. Consider this illustration: Giving donation to a deserving charity is a good work but a man wanting to show-off, if gives a donation to a charity and brags about it, may not qualify for Punya. The attitudes differ between these same-appearing deeds. The value of the so-called 'good-credit' or Punya accrued will be different, depending upon the intent. And indeed, these credits, good and bad, are not mutually cancelable. One has to face the consequences of both. One has to live through experiences consequent to both credits, of Paap and Punya. In other words, having done some Punya karma does not absolve one from effects of the Paap karma.

Karma

Karma is perhaps the best known term among all Hindu terminology. Karma literally means 'work' or 'work done' or 'action'. We all do 'karma' continuously every single moment. Everyone does karma. No one can spend a single moment without doing karma. Thinking too is karma and so is breathing. All karmas are actions and each action has its consequent reaction. Yields of Punya-karma are 'favourable' and those of Paap-karma are 'unfavourable'. Favourable or unfavourable they may appear to be but the consequences are certainly beneficial to the person if he learns from them and evolves further. Another very important understanding of the consequences of the karma is the fact that it cannot and should not be taken as 'punishment' or 'reward', though it might look like it. Yields from karma can accrue in a person's current life or in any forthcoming lives. It is inescapable, 'hard-wired' system, knowledge of which encourages people to do Punya-karma and avoid Paap-karma, sin.

The Bondage (Shackling) of Karma

One's present action, whatever it may be, binds one to its result. Cause is bound to effect. For having done any work, 'good' or 'bad', one has to live through (in this birth or the subsequent), experience of its results. Thus one is shackled in the cycle of doing work and then into taking subsequent births to 'suffer' (or 'enjoy') the consequences. This is the unending cycle of births and rebirths. An endless 'game'. This game can be over only when one stops working, or stops accruing the effects of work. As no one can stop 'working', the smart seeker of liberation or salvation, the follower of the Bhagavad Gita, knows the secret of working without being shackled thus escaping the trap of karma.

Salvation, Ultimate-goal, Liberation, Mukti or Brahm-Nirvan

Salvation is what no one seems to want unlike food and shelter. However, expanding on usual food-shelter and other mundane wants, man ultimately discovers the desire of desires. Anyone and everyone come face-to-face with this innate desire of obtaining freedom from all wants, the coveted liberartion. Liberation is one common desire, nay the most intense desire, among all of us. Whether identified as yet by one or not, this fact will emerge; and once it emerges, all the rest of desires become non-desires. Our desire for salvation is an inviolable truth. In the Hindu literature, salvation or the ultimate-goal-of-human is known by the terms, 'Mukti' or 'Moksha'. Sanskrit 'Mukti' is translated as liberation or freedom from wants. It is also referred to as 'Nirvan' or 'Brahm Nirvan'.

Karma decides the life. Punya-karma individual gets into 'favourable' situations and the Paap-karma individual, the 'unfavourable'. The words 'favourable' and 'unfavourable' are relative terms; what is meant by 'favourable' is 'appearing favourable to that individual at the given time'. However, the fact is that both the 'favourable' or 'unfavourable' circumstances, in which the individual finds himself, have occurred for development and evolution of that individuals, and are considered by Hindu philosophers as 'always favourable' and as 'always in the best interest' of that individual. Adversities are considered as best opportunities while good-times complacency has brought down many.

We have free choice. And using the cocktail of various life-parameters, a man acts. His action would define his future; now in his current life as well as his future births. The skill lies in what action one needs to do. The Gita unveils this secret, how to act so that it does not leave any reaction. And if one succeeds in performing without leaving any residual effect, he would succeed in attaining 'liberation' from wants as well as from the cycle of life and death and would become one with God; as He too is free from wants. Hindus do not say "Insha Allah" (God willing) as he knows that God is beyond wills, wishes and wants.

Who will achieve Moksha? Certainly not the sinner, that person who has done the Paap-karma and do not be surprised, but Hindu-philosophy explains that even the doer of Punya-karma will also not get the 'liberation'. The trick lies in understanding how to do the karma. This is the trick that we want to pick up from the Gita. And, therefore, the reading of the Bhagavad Gita is a must, where the God unfolds secrets and practical tips that can be used by anyone.

Once one knows this trick, he is in the state of 'liberation' or 'Mukti' and is said to have attained 'Moksha' or 'Nirvan' or 'Brahm-Nirvan'. We know that Lord Gautam Buddha achieved 'Nirvan' sitting under a tree during meditation in one flash of powerful thought. Among Hindus the word 'Brahm-Nirvan' is more common as compared to the word 'Nirvan'. Since Buddhism is an atheist religion, the Nirvan is a Buddhist, Godless-liberation whereas Brahm-Nirvan is Godly liberation. As Hindus believe that Buddha was an incarnation of Vishnu, they accept any of the above stated Nirvans as divine and are held in high esteem.

Death, Rebirth and Reincarnation

Rebirth, reincarnation, afterlife, immortal soul, transmigration of soul, spirit resurrection, Heaven, Hell, Day of Judgment, etc have fascinated all the people for all the time.

Death, though a sad occasion for the near and dear ones of the deceased on account of irreversible parting; a Hindu's perception of death is much less fearful. His philosophy assures continuity of life until one evolves to perfection: Death is not the end of life; it is a mere dropping of a curtain. When the curtain rises, one finds himself set on a new stage with a new scene more in line with what he desired and experienced earlier. The Bhagavad Gita does not demonise death; it is an opportunity, rebirth a mere change of the 'garment' (the body).

Not only Hindus but a majority of philosophies and religions believed that we reincarnate, albeit, Hindus were earliest, not only in its casual acknowledgement but it became a central tenet that gave rise to basic logic behind the morality and religion.

One finds in the works of Socrates, Pythagoras and Plato their overwhelming belief in rebirth. Even before the Greeks, their tormentors, the pagan Germanic tribe, the Teutons and, Asatru believed in the rebirth. Romans also believed it.

In their ancient faiths, the Egyptians, the African religions, Native American Indians, Inuit Eskimos, Norse Vikings, Celts, Anglo-Saxons, Aztec and Inca people believed in the rebirth.

The Kabbalists, following Orthodox Judaism, also base their religious ideas on rebirth; indeed the mainstream Judaism rejects the idea of reincarnation.

It is same with Islam, where the prominent tradition do not approve of the idea of reincarnation, their older traditions, especially what is now known as Sufism, subscribe to the idea of rebirth. Muslim scholar Ibn Rushd, who was banished by religious authorities, believed that humans had soul in two parts, one individual and other divine and is same through all humans, that it does not die, and is eternal.

Before getting purged during early history of Christianity, their literature had many references to reincarnation. Jesus himself may have believed in it. He asks the disciples if they recognized John the Baptist as Elijah reborn, who had lived some 900 years prior to John. Druze religion also has references of the reincarnation.

All of the eastern religions, Hinduism, Jainism, Taoism, Sikhism, etc believe in the rebirth in some or the other manner.

In case of Buddhism, it is a little confusing. According to Buddhism, there is no permanent and unchanging soul; therefore, there is the discussion as to what is transmitted between lives. In spite of the doctrinal beliefs against the idea of a soul, some Buddhists believe that a new-born child may be the reincarnation of someone dead earlier. Also there is a popular concept that by following the '8-fold path' one can reach 'Nirvan', the 'enlightenment' and escape the cycle of rebirth, hinting at existence of rebirth and life after death.

Mayan, Zoroastrian and Bahai do not mention about rebirth or reincarnation; their teachings however do have elements pointing to 'life' beyond death.

Ignoring the official teachings of the religions, if one was to investigate the phenomena of reincarnation, most people will perhaps agree as seen in the modern times in the work done by Thomas Huxley, Professor Ian Stevenson, Dr. Brian L Weiss,

Dr. Walter Semkiw, Jane, Peter Ramster, Edger Cayce, Rudolf Steiner and numerous others that the rebirth is not a myth but a provable proposition based on numerous well documented incidents. Theosophists and Gnostics too consider reincarnation as a matter of fact.

On birth, we come not empty-handed but armed with assets of all previous karmas and abilities of doing more karma in the current birth. Our traits such as temperament, likes, dislikes, opportunities and circumstances are the results of karma. Thus life is a vector equation of our previus and current karmas.

A person, well versed with Hindu concept of rebirth, knows that he should never give up his efforts even if it is a distant goal. Whatever karma will he do, will remain with him, it will not be wasted even at death. In his next birth, he will not be able to take Dollars or gold, but he will certainly take with him his karma. Hence he does not give up his karma, till death. He is constantly striving. Skills honed in current birth would be assets in the next.

Rebirth or not, all religions have an idea of something that happens after death. They may call it rebirth, reincarnation, after-life, the immortal soul, the transmigration of soul, Resurrection, Heaven, Hell or the Day of Judgment.

Heaven and Hell

Heaven and Hell mentioned in the Bhagavad Gita are completely different from what an average man having background of Bible or Koran will assume. Hindu heaven or hell is not a permanent place or a permanent situation. It is a part of karmic justice system and based on one's karma one will experience them for a certain time. In all probability, heaven and hell are no specific places; perhaps it is the heavenly or hellish experience during one's life cycles. Pleasant experiences are heaven and painful experiences are hell. Many believe the heaven and hell to be some of the 'worlds' among several strata of the 'worlds' specified in the Hindu literature. Indeed, in certain 'Purans' one does find mention of heaven and hell almost as depicted in the Abrahamic literature, but that depiction is generally taken by most Hindus as a simplistic view to keep the mankind from doing sinful, evil activity and turn him towards virtuous activities. In any case, it is not a permanent resting place. After exhausting the karma of 'Punya' (meritorious work) the righteous returns back from Heaven to the mortal world back into the cycle of births and deaths. Refer to the Gita 9-20, 21.

"May God Rest Him in Peace"

For Hindus, the life is evolution and it can end only upon liberation. Life does not end at the death. At death, his current body is shed for a newer body that is more suited for his further evolution. Somewhat similar but not as simple, the progress of an Undergraduate, who goes for Graduation and then for Masters. Upon death, for him, his well-wishers ideally wish: "May, God speed his journey to liberation (or to the ultimate truth)" instead of resting him in peace. One of the minor strains of Hindus does believe in good souls staying permanently in proximity of God, so it would not be wrong to say 'May his soul rest in peace', but knower of the Bhagavad Gita would use the former wish, as why should he wish for blocking the progress of the dead man towards true salvation.

Cremation of Dead

Hindus gererally consign their dead to fire. However there are some exceptions too; very young children and monks are not cremated but are usually buried. Of late, many followers of other religions too have begun opting for cremation as a preferred method out of the advantages they have notice; minimal use of land, same spot can be used for all cremations irrespective of caste, creed or social status, incineration of germs along with the body and elimination of dangers from grave desecration.

It is believed that Lord Shiv is alwalys present on the cremation ground, thus invariably all Hindu cremation grounds bear His temples, where he lovingly accepts his child who has returned to him from the mortal world.

Cremation rituals involve almost a poetic balance between grief of the loss of loved one and the need to face the truth' it is incumbent upon none other but the son of the deceased to light the fire. Subsequent ot cremation, close relatives generally observe rituals for next 13 days and thereafter once a year memorial ceremony, known as 'Shraddha' is held.

Soul, Atma, Atman, Jivatma and Jivatman

These are some of the commonly employed terms in Hinduism. It is generally understood by most of the people around the world that we all have a soul in our body. That is Atma (same as

Atman). Atma in a body is known as Jivatma or Jivatman (Jiv-individual life form). Atma is also described as 'self' because it is the true-self of the body in which it resides and continues even after his death in next birth (next-body).

Supersoul, Paramatma, Parmatman

Paramatma is super-soul, the one shared by all. It is in everyone's body and is connected with everyone. Practically, Hindus consider Paramatma as God for ease of understanding and some sort of conceptual quantification of the entity of God, although in the truer sense it is the Brahman that is akin to God, the creator of everything including Atma, Paramatma, the whole universe (Brahmand).

To make connection between these three terms, Atma, Paramatma and Brahman, consider a vivid example given in the Upanishadic texts: Two birds are sitting on a tree. The tree is the Jiva (life-form); one bird is the Atma that eats the fruit of the tree; the second bird, who merely watches as a witness, is the Paramatma. The Brahman is everything; the tree, the birds and the system. The God.

God, Brahm, Brahman, Absolute, Eternal, Ultimate Reality

Brahm is same as Brahman. Take care not to misunderstand 'Brahm' or 'Brahman' that is akin to God, with other similar sounding words; 'Brahma' or 'Brahmin'. Both these are completely different from Brahm and Brahman and exchanging one word for the other would lead to massive misunderstanding. This possibility of misunderstanding exists in English writing as the spellings of these words are very close. In the mother language Sanskrit, there is no scope of mistake as their spellings differ, being phonetically arranged.

'Brahm' or 'Brahman' is the Ultimate Reality, the God and all its creation, everything. Expressions 'Absolute', 'Eternal' and 'Ultimate Reality,' etc are also used for God.

Brahman is indefinable but if it has to be stated, it could be said to be the unchanging, infinite, immanent, and transcendent reality and which is the divine foundation of all matter, energy, time, space, being, and everything beyond in this universe. The nature of Brahman is described differently by philosophers as transpersonal, personal and impersonal.

Hinduism believes that God cannot be described by any amount of verbiage. It is un-fathomable by any human instrument. All the religions of the world believe this truth that is experienced by the seekers. Vedas and Upanishads have again and again specified this truth.

Aum, Om, ॐ

This monosyllable is a sacred first alphabet of Sanskrit language and also an expression of God. There are hundreds of other spiritual attributes assigned to the monosyllable Aum, described in ancient literature. In brief, 'Aum' (also written by some as 'Om'), signifies God or Brahm, Brahman or Supreme Being—an entity that includes everything manifest or unmanifest in this universe. It is said to be an embodiment of the essence of all Vedas; compressed in the symbol of Aum. This symbol is endowed with occult powers of the highest character. For ease of quick understanding read Supreme Being or God wherever 'Aum' word occurs.

Maya (Delusion)

The word 'Maya', as it appears in the Gita, refers to the delusion of mind. It is Maya or delusion, that makes us see, believe and feel what is unreal, to be real and the vice versa. Fixed, non-moving image in the frames of the film appear moving in cinema. Maya creates a make-believe world around us. It brings man to want evil things by making them appear to be good and discard beneficial things. It is said to deceive everyone. Only true knowledge can uncover the truth that is veiled by the Maya, just as a stick in water seems bent, until we acquire the knowledge of refraction phenomena.

Non-Fatalisticism

Many have described Hinduism and Hindus to be fatalistic, that a man is helplessly tied to his destiny or fate. Some say that a man is but a toy in the hands of God, he dances at the tunes and script made by God. Some also say that a man is born with a destiny and nothing can be done except to live it out. These views are nothing but an aberration, a mistake, at best opinions of the ignorant, since it completely overlooks the free-will and karma factor. In this sense, Hinduism stands completely away from other religions, where the misdeeds are sometimes blamed on circumstances or Satan. Vedas and Gita unequivocally declare that one is responsible for one's acts (Karma). Role of fate is accepted but in its ranking it is well below that of karma. The Gita, 18-14, ascribes the last (5th) rank to fate among the causes for the action. One has to own up his responsibility, one cannot escape his karma. One can change one's 'future' or 'fate' by indulging in greater karma of desirable nature. This genius of karma system is designed for man's evolution. Blaming circumstance or fate for the ills will make him blind towards his own accountability and scuttle his evolution. A fair-minded Hindu, or for that matter anyone else, will always try to improve his karma record for better dividends in his life.

A smart follower of Karma Philosophy would act in a cleaver way: disown rewards of 'good' karma and own up 'rewards' of 'bad' karma. A person having mastered the teachings of the Gita would disown the rewards of all his karmas, bad or good.

In actual practice, people do say: 'whatever is in my fate will happen' or some more philosophical kinds say: 'Everything happens as per God's wish, without his wish nothing can happen, not even a leaf of a tree can move'. And some more devoted types would say: 'As God willed'. These kinds of things are spoken by all people at all times across all the religions; even many Hindus too say this. But those who followthe Gita will say it differently. They would not be uttering those sentences that smack of helplessness. They would say, 'Whatever happens is meant for my own good and for my own development, I have to learn from it and emerge more mature, physically, mentally, and spiritually, from it.' One cannot escape one's karma, but one can change one's ways, can do better karma. A fair-minded Hindu would always try to improve his or her karma record when seeking improvements in his life.

Miracles

Prophet Mohammad candidly said that he could not do miracles, that he was against the idea of miracles, thus in the main-stream Islam we do not notice too much of miracle-mongering. Quite the opposite, in Christianity, miracles are the foundation of the religion. It began with the birth of Jesus Christ. A Christian saint[26] is no saint if he or she has not performed miracles. Indeed, the Sufi form of Islam does revolve around miracles.

Hindu faith has both the elements; the Bhakti oriented (Love-oriented) worshippers who are somewhat equivalent to Sufi-Islam or to Christianity, does have a lot of elements of miracles, while the Jnan oriented (Knowledge-oriented) worshippers and karma-oriented (Action-oriented) worshippers consider miracles as unnecessary and as an inferior tool for strengthening their faith in God. In the life of Lord Rama, there are no miracles where as in Lord Krishna's life there is a string of miracles beginning from His birth.

Travelling in India will take one face-to-face with literally thousands of stories of miracles; cure from incurable diseases, miraculous help coming from unknown, extraordinary visions,

26 There are certain rules that have to be fulfilled before Vatican canonises sainthood; a number of proven and witnessed miracles being one of them.

etc. Behind many temples, water holes, mountains, caves, etc. one finds stories of miracles, making them venerated places. In this world every individual has some or other problem and he seeks help from every description of healers; where the role of medical intervention is closed, he goes for the miracle-route. Therefore, it should not surprise anyone to see people thronging the miracle-men and miracle-sites.

All miracles can be separated in 3 parts to do a further analysis.

Some happen by divine intervention. These happen automatically. They have highest value.

Some happen by wish of a holy person, who out of his love and sympathy will cause the miracle. These miracles are somewhat questionable.

The third variety of miracles can be performed by an expert tantric. A Hath-Yogi or a tantrik can do miracles using certain spiritual techniques. Tantrik-driven miracles are said to have on several occasions, eventually harmed the performer and even the benefactor due to its injudicious application. Most mainstream mystics and spiritual persons are seen to keep away from that sort of tantrik techniques. It is not a mainstream Yoga due to its 'bad name' and questionable (mis) use. Tantrik techniques, besides in India, have been used by many all over the world due to its perceived value in obtaining undue benefit on one hand and for harming the adversary on the other hand. Mayans, Aztecs, Egyptians, etc also have used this 'evil' knowledge.

It is told in scriptures that after practising genuine love towards mankind and thereby having cleansed the soul, anyone can reach a stage known as 'Vaachaa Siddhi'. Whatever you speak will happen.

A true holy person knows that the miracles bring fame and fame will come in his way of spiritual progress. Fame is an entrapment, potentially most powerful among all distractions, for a God seeker to get diverted from path to God. It is said to be comparable to a game of 'snake-and-ladder' where the 'fame' will take the seeker almost reaching 'home' (God) down the 'snake', pushed behind by years or even many lives depending upon what damage the fame has been able to inflict upon him.

Among Hindu saints, many have apologized to God and even requested Him to take away their ability of doing miracles. In Hinduism, it is not considered meritorious to perform miracles and thereby impress followers. And for genuine God-seekers, this ability comes in their way in the form of disturbance from the people trying to use and misuse saint's divine ability for their selfish motives. There are many cases when in the fit of extreme sympathy, sometimes some saints have brought the dead to life and thereafter having realized its implications, they have offered themselves for punishment for the 'crime of meddling in the affairs of God'. Even some of them have self-punished themselves by death in some recorded cases. As a matter of fact, most Hindus see the miracles as undesirable interference into God's working.

Miracles that we common men understand are considered by the knowledgeables as non-miracles. They would, on the other hand, want people to notice the great genuine miracles that are actually happening every moment around us, to which we are oblivious and thereby instead of going for the creator of those great miracles, we foolishly go after the creators of petty-miracles. Aren't these miracles, this cosmos, the rising sun suspended by itself, the fragrance of a flower, the first breathing of a child after birth, the memory, the life? These are the kind of miracles that will help us go near the God, the other miracles may not.

Yog (Yoga)

In the Bhagavad Gita every chapter is known as Yog. An average person knows Yog to be a fitness tool and physical exercise.

That the Yog is a physical fitness tool is not incorrect but it is not its complete meaning. English word 'Yoke' (Meaning: 'to join'; a horse is yoked to the cart) is same as Sanskrit 'Yog' and also means the same, 'to join'. But in the Gita or in the spiritual context, the word Yog generally means 'to join with God or divinity. Words 'yoke' and 'Yog' are both derived from ancient Sanskrit root word 'Yuj' meaning 'to join'.

Lord Krishna is described severally in the Bhagavad Gita, but importantly, is addressed as Yogeshwar, the 'God of Yog' or 'God of Yogis' by prince Arjun.

Yog is thus the 'science or knowledge of how to unite with God' or 'the practice of uniting with God' or 'the method of uniting with God'.

All Chapters are Yog in the Bhagavad Gita

Because the Bhagavad Gita teaches one as to how to join one's own self with divinity, it is also known as 'Yog Shashtra' and all of its chapters are given their names as one or the other kind of Yog.

List of Sanskrit Names of all Chapters (All are Yogas, Yogs)

Chapter 1	Arjun-Vishad-Yog
Chapter 2	Sankhya-Yog
Chapter 3	Karma-Yog
Chapter 4	Gnyan-Karma-Sanyas-Yog
Chapter 5	Karma-Sanyas-Yog
Chapter 6	Atma-Saynyam-Yog
Chapter 7	Gnyan-Vignyan-Yog
Chapter 8	Akshar-Brahm-Yog
Chapter 9	Raj-Vidya-Raj-Guhya-Yog
Chapter 10	Vibhuti-Yog
Chapter 11	Viswa-Rup-Darshan-Yog
Chapter 12	Bhakti-Yog
Chapter 13	Kshetra-Kshetragnya-Vibhag-Yog
Chapter 14	Guna-Treya-Vibhag-Yog

Chapter 15	Purushottam-Yog
Chapter 16	Daivasur-Sampad-Vibhag-Yog
Chapter 17	Shraddha-Treya-Vibhag-Yog
Chapter 18	Moksha-Sanyas-Yog

Yajna, Sacrifice, Selfless Service

'Yajna' word appears many times in the Bhagavad Gita, as one of the most important terms. It is variously translated as "self-less service', 'fire-ritual' or as 'sacrifice', where the performing priests offer food (coconut, rice, ghee[27], milk, etc) to the holy fire and in return asks Gods for whatever is desired by him (peace, happiness, strength, victory, children, rain, etc) by chanting appropriate sacred verses. This understanding is not wrong but is incomplete and misleading. Some people have translated the word 'Yajna' as the 'sacrifice'. The self-less work is indeed a sacrifice. This meaning is not untrue but lacks full import because, to many who are from other religions, the word sacrifice mostly indicates ritual-sacrificing (slaughtering) of an animal (akin to Islamic Qurbani). These are not the 'Yajnas' that are referred to by the creator of the Gita.

The Vedic-Yajna was primarily a self-less service, done by a dedicated group of people, sacrificing-self-interest, even inviting inconvenience and discomfort for the upliftment of the society, and importantly, done in a very sincere spirit as worship of God. The word 'Yajna' appearing at several places in the Gita, generally means, 'self-less service' or 'work done in the spirit of self-less service' or 'God's work' or more accurately, 'the work done in the same spirit as done by God' (because God works selflessly). Broadly but very truly, any work done with a main purpose of self-less service is termed as 'Yajna', including even a day-to-day activities if done in the spirit of selfless act.

27 Clarified Butter

If one studies, teaches, feeds, cures or helps others, without expecting any return, has known to have performed 'Yajna.' It is for this that God has referred to Yajna as Dravya-Yajna, Tapo-Yajna, Yog-Yajna, Jnan-Yajna and Swadhyay-Yajna at 4-25, 28: "Some yogis perform the service of worship to Devas, while others study scriptures for self-knowledge. Some restrain their senses and give up their sensual pleasures. Others perform breathing and other yogic exercises. Some give charity and offer their wealth as a sacrifice. And some toil in the study of the self".

Yajna is, therefore, a very powerful tool for human upliftment, when deployed in its true spirit.

The word 'Yajna' is also derived from the root word 'Yuj', the same root as what gave us the word 'yog', 'yoga'. Having derived from 'Yuj', it is spelled as 'Yajna'.

'Yuj' in Yajna has three-fold meaning; to unite, to worship and to befriend. Yajna done with the Vedic procedures would yield these three-fold benefits for the mankind in the vicinity of the location of the Yajna. The spirit in its performance is the self-less love for the mankind, love for God and desire to help the fellow human beings.

Selfless Yajnas when performed in those regions where population is ignorant, deprived and thereby leading sub-human lives, bring to them the benefits of advanced civilization with which they can build their life that balances worldly-enjoyments with spiritual development and with which they begin to value discipline, the self-restraint, control over baser desires, acquire medicinal knowledge to fight ailments, learn hygiene, language and development of various skills.

Popular forms of ritualistic Yajnas can be divided in two groups, most important and what is referred as 'self-less-sacrifice' in the Gita are those that are done for human upliftment. The other types of ritualistic Yajnas are performed for achieving some worldly gain or a favour from Gods. These kinds of Yajnas are performed for good progeny, wealth, etc.

Reading the Gita, one realizes that we all are required to do nothing else but Yajna and Yajna alone at all times. That only is the answer to all the problems mankind faces today. Clearly, it has been spelled at 3-10,11,12,13: "In the beginning Lord Prajapati (Lord Brahma, the creator among the trinity of Gods) created human beings by selfless service (Yajna) and said: By selflessly serving (by Yajna) each other you shall prosper and the sacrificial service (Yajna) shall fulfil all your desires. Nourish the Celestial Controllers (Devas; essence of air, rain, seas, earth, and similar hundreds of others that 'control' the happenings around us) with selfless service (Yajna), and they will nourish you. Thus nourishing one another you shall attain the Supreme goal. The Celestial Controllers, served by selfless service (Yajna), will give you all desired objects. One who enjoys the gift of Devas without sharing with others is, indeed, a thief. The righteous ones who eat after feeding others are freed from all sins, but the impious who cook food only for themselves without first offering to God, or sharing with others verily eats sin."

And in the non-performance of Yajna, the selfless service, God cautions us in the 4-31: "Those who perform selfless service (Yajna) obtain the nectar of Self-knowledge as a result of their sacrifice and attain the Supreme Being. O, Arjun, even this world is not a happy place for the non-sacrificer, how can the other world be?"

Swastik and the Aryan Connection

Swastik is a 'Good Luck' sign of Hindus. It was also used by the ancient Germanic tribes of pre-Christian era in Europe. With its identity considered as 'Aryan' it had been adopted by the Nazi Germany in 20th century for rousing the patriotic-passion among Germans by Adolf Hitler. Due to its adoption by Nazis, this divine sign of Hindus is occasionally misunderstood even if applied in context of Hindus. For Hindus, this is a purely a religious, non-political 'good-luck' symbol. Rudyard Kipling (1835-1936), a Mumbai-born English writer and recipient of the 1907 Nobel Prize in literature, used to inscribe the Swastik and the picture of Hindu God Ganesh on his books. Even he had to take Swastik off his books lest he gets identified with Nazis.

Not only had Hitler misappropriated the Swastik symbol, he also had a very different idea of the term 'Aryan'. For him, Aryan meant a race that was tall, fair, having blue eyes and blonde hair. His obsession with developing this 'super-race' resulted in physical destruction of rest of the people, the Jews, Gypsies, and others who would not fit the physical description of his 'super-race'.

Arya and Aryan are Sanskrit words. Sanskrit is considered as the mother language of all the Indo-European languages and in it the word Aryan is always used as an adjective signifying 'cultured person' or a 'noble man' and on many occasions the term is used for addressing husband, akin to saying 'hubby' or 'dear'. Never was it used as a term to signify a particular race. Due to mistakes of early European historians, 'Arya' word came to denote a race which was never there to begin with. As a lot of water has passed under the bridge it is difficult to correct the incorrect at this time, however, if the truth is known, it will help distancing 'Nazi-Aryan' of Hitler from a benign original Sanskrit Aryan referred to in Hinduism.

As for the Arya Migration theory, there are two different versions held by different historians. First version which was popular until recently made Central Asian mountains as the place from where 'Aryan race' spread across to Europe and India. Another version based on newer findings using newer research techniques and tools state India as the origin of 'Aryans', from where they migrated to other parts of the world. Not only thousands of words of European language have been traced to have their roots in Sanskrit, but even their grammar has been traced to Sanskrit. In the Vedic texts, India is described at innumerable places as the 'Aryavarta', meaning the abode of Aryas, further reinforcing the newer research that places Aryan as original inhabitants of India (and not having been migrated from Central Asia). Historians have however not yet found unanimity as to where really the Aryans originated, but the mass of the evidences on the new theory is mounting and before long the existing migration theory may have to be reconsidered. Suffice here to understand that Nazism and their concept of Aryan race have nothing to do with Arya adjective used in India. The word Aryan thus has nothing to do with race. And that the Swastik is a 'Good Luck' sign for Hindus. It is a purely religious, non-political 'good-luck' symbol and most importantly, there never was an invasion of 'Aryans' on Dravidians. Both were original inhabitants of ancient India.

Deva

Devas find frequent mention in the Bhagavad Gita. Devas are also known as the 'Celestial Controllers' controlling essence of natural phenomena such as wind, sun, moon, rain, fire, etc. They are also referred in some translations as 'Demi-Gods'. They are divine beings and said to be possessor of brilliant qualities as described in the Gita 16-1, 2, 3: "Fearlessness, purity of inner psyche, perseverance in the yoga of self-knowledge, charity, sense restraint, sacrifice (selfless service, Yajna), study of the scriptures, austerity, honesty; non-violence, truthfulness, absence of anger, renunciation, equanimity, abstaining from back-biting or malicious talk, compassion for all creatures, freedom from greed, gentleness, modesty, absence of fickleness, splendour, forgiveness, fortitude, cleanliness, absence of malice, and absence of pride these are some of the qualities of those endowed with Deva (divine) virtues, O, Arjun."

Yaksha, Gandharva, Vanar, Nag

These are said to be the individuals who are part-human and part-divine or part-human and part-animal or even a combination of all, finding their mention in the Bhagavad Gita. Yaksha and Gandharva are said to be inhabitants of higher worlds, above the plane of human world. These have certain characteristics and abilities that differentiate them from humans, although they may look like humans. Kuber, a Yaksha is treasurer of Devas.

Vanar (meaning monkey) and Nag (meaning serpent or snake) referred to in the Gita are thought to be human tribes possessing specific traits and abilities. Lord Hanuman was a Vanar, who is supposed to be a protector of the chariot of Arjun in the war of Mahabharata and finds his mention in the Gita at 1-20, stating his prime position on the flag of Arjun. Interestingly, Lord Hanuman is considered to have a very long life and is still believed to be alive[28] along with six more individuals.

Satan, Shaitan

In contrast to the Christian and Islamic traditions, Hinduism does not recognize existence of any central evil force, agency or entity such as the Satan, Shaitan or Devil that opposes God. Hindu logic explains that everyone of us have within ourselves 'good' and 'bad' tendencies. Excess of bad tendency makes a person devilish and that of good makes him good-angelic. Both tendencies are God created and it depends on the individual who deploys them.

'Bad' bombing on Hiroshima and Nagasaki brought an end to the world war, a desirable 'good' outcome. What is bad and what is good becomes difficult to judge.

28 In the scriptures they have stated names of seven individuals who have long life and they are believed to be alive till date. They are Ashwathama (son of guru Drona), Bali (Danav Mahabali), Vyas (Author of the Bhagavad Gita), Krup (Guru of Kauravs), Parashuram (Considered an incarnation of Lord Vishnu), Hanuman (Famed as Lord Rama's care taker and having sharp intellect with legendary physical strength) and Vibhishan (Youngest brother of Rakshas Ravan).

Satan is said to be tempting people. The entire commercial world, publicity firms and media do nothing except enticing the people. Hindus believe that an attraction is your own state of mind. 'The beauty lies in the eyes of the beholder'.

Hindus consider the whole world to be beautiful and everything therein to be good. Perhaps the way God felt as expressed in the Biblical literature: "God saw all that he had made, and it was very good" (Gn 1:31).

Asur, Rakshas, Danav and Daitya

Asurs, Rakshas,' Danav and Daitya are mentioned in the Hindu literature. They are not Satan, but they bear closest description in terms of the traits that are identified with Satan.

At 16-4, Gita describes their traits: "The marks of those who are born with Asuric qualities are: Hypocrisy, arrogance, pride, anger, harshness, and ignorance". Asurs, Rakshas, Danavs and Daityas like to appear to be 'good' people and therefore they may do a lot of 'good appearing' work, however, the difference becomes visible when their self-interest is at stake. In terms of priority it is 'me, mine and myself' at any cost.

Satan is considered as 'anti-God' but Asurs, Rakshas', Danavs and Daityas are not identified as 'against God'; quite to the contrary, they go to God with even more vigor than ordinary believers, however always, with the selfish motive of material profit. They try to monopolize God by dissuading others from worshipping Him; instead demanding from folks that looking to their might, the folks should worship them instead of God.

Interestingly, however, some members of Asurs, Rakshas', Danavs and Daityas have been extremely divine and God-loving. In the Gita, Lord Krishna acknowledges those great souls by naming Prahalad, who was son of a Danav, as His embodiment. Scriptures have decorated many Asurs and Danavs with respect. When they turned evil or dangerous to the society in the course of fulfilling their lust or grandeur, they fell from the grace. Ravan and Maha Bali stand tall among those decorated. Ravan had created many Ragas after extensive study; he was an expert astronomer who could accurately chart stars and planets, an accomplished astrologer, his kingdom was one of the most scientifically and materially advanced in his times and even said to have possessed airplanes. He stood disgraced later on and held in contempt because he lived an immoral life and because he had lustily kidnapped wife of Lord Rama. Similarly, Maha Bali was an Asur, who had cared for his public and ensured that every citizen was provided 'food-shelter-education'. To remember his contribution to the society, the 2nd day after the New Year[29] is named 'Bali-Pratipada' after him. Also one more major festival, Onam[30], is celebrated in the Indian state of Kerala on lines of Diwali to respectfully remember him. However, he was exiled to nether world by Vaman, an incarnation of God Vishnu, as a punishment for his injudicious behaviour and inadvertent damage he inflicted on society by undermining role of austerities, discipline and sacrifice. He still has high reputation and he is said to be actually alive and makes an appearance to his dear 'subjects', the people of Kerala on every Onam; a one-day parole per year granted by God while sending him off to nether world! Famous Mahabalipuram temple of Tamil Nadu is testimony to his towering personality.

Asur teacher, a Brahmin sage known as Shukracharya stands tall as the top-most educator in the Hindu scriptures. He is said to be superior in certain disciplines even to Brihaspati, the teacher of Devas. In the Gita, Lord Krishna acknowledges them both for their own excellence.

29 2nd day of the Hindu month of Kartik is celebrated as Bali-Pratipada. For many Hindus, 1st Kartik is the New Year. (Many other Hindus consider 1st Chaitra as New Year instead of 1st Kartik).

30 Onam is celebrated on the birth anniversary of God Vaman, (12th Bhadrapad month-Aug-Sep time) who was responsible for exiling the Danav Mahabali to the nether world. Can there be a better way to acknowledge noble yet a misguided Danav.

Thus, the Asurs, Rakshas', Danavs and Daityas are considerably different entities in Hinduism than the Satan in other faiths.

Temples are not Hindu Churches (or Mosques or Synagogues)

The Hindu temple is different from other places of worship, because they contain in them an invoked deity. In the temple you are in presence of a living God from whom you can derive inspiration to become a better person, to say 'thank you', to confess, and to ask for help.

Because the God is invoked (by the religious ceremony of 'Pran-Pratistha' meaning, 'life instilling'), they are not easily founded. They cannot be constructed mindlessly at any place without due considerations. Temples are neither lightly founded nor can they be easily relocated by the followers.

Besides worshipping of God, the temples have also another role to play. It is a community centre where people can meet, celebrate festivals, take care of underprivileged, learn scriptures and obtain advice on spiritual matters.

Music, Singing, Dance and Drama

Music is considered very essential to human development. One entire Veda, the Sam-Veda, is dedicated to music. Music, singing, dance, drama and all the forms of art are intrinsically connected. Lord Shiv is known as patron of this discipline, earning Him a name, 'Nataraj' (Nataraj=Most proficient Artist). Lord Shiv is always shown with a musical instrument 'Damru'[31] in his hand.

Hinduism is unthinkable without music, singing and dancing. Lord Krishna and his flute and Goddess Saraswati and her Veena[32] are inseparable. Without a colourful floor-decoration, known as Rangoli, a festival is unthinkable in India.

---

31 Damru is a hand-held 2-sided small drum instrument.

32 Veena is a string instrument.

Music, dance, drama and art are part of Hindu worship. In this aspect it differs with Abrahamic faiths. Islam forbids music and Christianity though allows music, other art-forms are not part of their worship procedures. Hindu religious ceremonies include all the elements of art. On everyday basis, music, singing and drawing are employed in temples and private worship. While most temples always have some or the other musical instruments, many celebrated temples such as Somanath temple have a dedicated area with dance floor.

Vegetarianism

To be a vegetarian or to be a non-vegetarian is the topic, hotly debated, with supporters of each side taking strong positions, sometimes not even fully knowing the facts.

Traditionally, man was mainly vegetarian, eating easily available fruits and herbs but also eating meat occasionally on special days after a prize hunt. Some very small populace was almost completely non-vegetarian on account of their stay on remote barren near-polar regions; on the other hand, there was a large populace who were totally vegetarians. In the era of animal farming, cold-stores, refrigerators and transport systems, the use of meat has increased and it has become more common.

Both diets have their own merits and hence choice has to be made intellectually for one's own self. Most Hindu spiritual leaders and modern-day health-food-enthusiasts have advocated vegetarianism as being a preferred health diet, in a world that is predominantly meat-eater and meat-eating professing.

Freedom-loving Hinduism does not proscribe any food (save a few exceptions, discussed in this book). One can eat what suits best to him. Here comes the place for reason and judgment. Calories, minerals, vitamins, fibers, etc are available in different amounts and qualities in each item and thereby every food has certain specific property. We all decide what to eat based on what we like to eat as well as what we need to eat. Man, with free will, can make up his mind as he does on many other matters during his life.

Everyone knows that the protein bearing meats also have a high fat content and zero fiber content, contrasting with most carb intensive vegetables that have less fat and high fiber content.

In the Hinduism, thinkers have gone beyond these attributes of food. Not only it has considered the food value in terms of its nourishing ability, but how the food in itself as well as its preparation affects the minds and body of the people involved in preparing, cultivating, cooking and consuming of the food. Let us consider some of these aspects.

BODY-BUILDING PROTEINS, ENERGY SUPPLIER CARBS

We need proteins to build our body and the carbohydrates to provide the energy. The meat is rich in proteins and vegetables have plenty of carbohydrates. But these are not mutually exclusive attributes. For instance, vegetables also have proteins apart from the carbohydrates, and meats do have very energetic fat content. Advocates of non-vegetarian food say that the vegetarian diet does not have enough protein and protine deficient meal makes for smaller growth, smaller built and a weaker man, little realizing that the biggest and the mightiest animals roaming the world are vegetarians; the elephant, the horse, the rhino, the bull, the giraffe, etc. On the other hand, the non-vegetarian animals have always been smaller built.

Proponents of meat eating have indicated towards physically heavier and taller built people who consume meat when compared to the vegetable eating people, however, later researchers have also shown that heavier bodies and tallness has increased man's susceptibility to diseases, infections, bone damage and reduced agility, thus the 'better-built' man is not an unqualified advantage. Many scientists and leaders have been of small to medium built. Also many meat-promoters overlook the need for reduced protein intake after certain age when excess protein harms the body by taxing the liver and kidney.

Proteins decay faster. Protein intensive meat, fish, cooked lentils, cooked kidney-beans, etc cannot remain good for consumption beyond certain time without refrigeration. Vegetables with lesser protein can stay longer without refrigeration. The uncooked food-grains such as wheat, rice, corn, etc stay good for years without refrigeration.

Even a slightly stale meat can spread disease among humans because the germs that affect an animal can also affect the humans with equal ease. Whereas, generally speaking the germs that affect plant does not afflict a human with the same ease. Therefore, the cases of food-poisoning are minimal from vegetarian diet, and none whatsoever from mad-cow disease. Thus health risks are naturally minimized for a vegetarian.

ANATOMICAL CONSIDERATIONS

Nature has produced two kinds of animals; judged from the length of their intestines; those that have long intestine and those who have short intestines. Cows, goats, horses, elephants, humans, etc have long intestines. Lions, tigers, dogs, cats, etc have short intestines. Under natural environment, those animals that have long intestines prefer vegetarian food and those possessing shorter intestines eat meats.

Meats are processed faster in the animal body as their amino-acids are almost similar to those found in human cells. Meat eating animals need to discharge waste products as soon as digestion is complete and their short intestine helps throw away faeces faster. On the other hand, vegetarian diet being cellulosic, and much different than human cells, it needs longer to digest, necessitating a longer processing and therefore a longer intestine.

When a vegetarian animal (usually human) consumes meat, after its quick digestion and assimilation, its waste product remains stored in the intestine until it passes through the entire length, leading to toxicity in the lower intestine and the rectum. Meat eating humans, therefore, risk cancers and other rectum-centric diseases. Medical records point to high prevalence of such diseases among those humans who are strong meat consumers.

Promoters of meat-eating commonly point out to the presence of canine teeth in human mouth to prove that humans are supposed to be meat-eaters, mistakenly assuming that canines are needed only for tearing meat and not for tearing vegetarian foods. Sugar cane, for instance, and a host of other uncooked fruits and vegetables need canines, especially in absence of knife, etc tools.

If one was to observe animals drinking the water, one will find that those who are naturally vegetarian normally suck the water using their lips, just as we humans do. On the other hand, those animals who consume meat lick the water with their tongues.

Above stated factors are obvious, demonstrable and point to man's natural food as 'mainly-vegetables and fruits' like our closest relative, the monkey. However, Hinduism accepts that we humans, having been endowed with intelligence and creativity, can romance with other foods for our benefit, as long as we prefer or we like to indulge.

Hinduism has other much more important reasons to consider before summarizing whether to prefer a vegetarian diet or a non-vegetarian diet.

MORE IMPORTANT ASPECTS OF FOOD

Man does not live on food alone. Human development, art, culture, morality, economics, etc a play vital role, once man's basic need of filling his belly is fulfilled. A culturally advanced man likes to go beyond the basics and investigates if there are any plus-values beyond stomach-gratification or body-gratification to be obtained from food that he consumes. Ancient Hindus, therefore, considered many food-linked human tendencies and how best to utilize them in the process of human development.

Consider the cultural development. Nomadic herdsmen who move from place to place in search of green pastures for their cattle-rearing cannot produce a sustained quality culture due to their constant travels compared to what is possible for steady settled peoples. Agrarian societies create great cultures. Kalidas, Vyas and Valmiki could not be born among nomads; neither could they produce Shakuntalas, Mahabharatas or Ramayans. With explicit deliberation on this point, the ancient Hindu sages first taught the nomadic tribes to do farming and founded agriculture-based society, taught them virtues of vegetarianism and made them to settle at one place. In promoting vegetarianism, Vedic sages had done a lot of work during 'pre-historic' times. First step was to turn man from being a cannibal, and then move him to be a benign carnivorous to ultimately a benign herbivorous. This transformation has come about through a Herculean effort by a number of sages because it is not easy to overcome temptations of meat eating and remain herbivorous (vegetarian). It is in homage to those sages when vegetarians continue to stay that way and certainly those sages would be delighted to get new converts.

Consider now the moral angle. Many ancient Hindu sages, who had love for this world in their hearts, were so sensitive that they considered it a theft when flesh of an animal was taken without its permission. These sages and their followers consumed only the naturally fallen fruit of the tree. They still lived brilliant lives and were not malnourished.

Consider extension of sustainance potential of earth and its atmosphere. Man needs lesser land to sustain to be a vegetarian.

Veg-diet will help resource of the world to last longer. Vegetation is the primary resource; its derivative meat is a processed, secondary resource. Tons of vegetation gets converted into just a few pounds of flesh, sufficient feed for a smaller number of people as compared to direct consumption of same quantity of vegetation that can support thousand-fold more people. Consequently, earth resource is less stretched by vegetarians.

Recent studies made by environmentalists suggest that rearing cattle gives rise to greenhouse gases that negatively impacts the climate. Nobel awardee Dr. Rajendra Pachauri[33], who is himself a vegetarian, has recommended that every man should give up eating meat at least once a week and should progressively reduce meat consumption to save our planet.

In its economic dimension, as it is much cheaper to stay vegetarians, it makes more economic sense. Not only the cost of the non-veg food is higher, the cost of its preservation is significantly higher; whether live or dead.

Sensitizing: Slaughtering of the animals necessarily demands a certain in-sensitizing of mind; without which the slayer cannot undertake his task. He has to learn to see-not a scared, crying and struggling animal trying to save itself from the buthcher's knife. George Bernard Shaw (1856-1950), the famous British playwright, said once: "The worst sin towards our fellow creatures is not to hate them, but to be indifferent to them, that's the essence of inhumanity". The staff of the abbatoir has to become indifferent to the cattle, to the animal who has eyes, ears like us humans and who behaves also just the same. Even the consumer of the meat too learns indifference. Haven't we read at many places that even a staunch non-vegetarian turns into vegetarian, if he visits the slaughter house and witnesses blood-chilling cruelty? Vegetarian he remains, albeit till he regains his 'practised-insensitivity of years'.

33 Dr. Rajendra Pachauri won the Nobel Peace Prize in 2007 along with former US Vice President Al Gore.

A survey was conducted among the jailbirds of Mumbai to correlate food-habits versus the nature of the crime. It emerged that non-vegetarians had a significant lead in the category of 'very heinous crimes'.

However, despite all these overwhelming indications towards vegetarianism, Hindus do not propose ban on non-vegetarian food, in fact, they need it to exist as a choice. Should we, as a rule, impart sensitivity among all? At what point the education of sensitivity should end? When we walk, talk and do things, a lot of microbes die around us. As everyone knows, the plants too have life, why is it okay to cut an obergine from its plant? What happens in the nature all the time? Animals are not hunted by other animals? And what about meat harvested by humane means, can it not be allowed if some prefer it?

Can we afford a sensitive soldier who shudders killing the enemy? Will he be able to fight wars and defend his country? What should a police officer do when he confronts a gun wielding thug, should he show him mercy? Buddhist kingdoms of the past, which had practised unbalanced non-violence, lost their kingdoms and territories when enemies attacked. Afghanistan, Pakistan, Indonesia, Bangladesh, Malaysia, Western Tibet are living testimonies, of once thriving centres of Buddhism, now stripped of it as they failed to stand up to the sword-weilding attackers. Those parts of the world, that followed Vedic Hindu traditions, could somewhat resist, as seen in as yet Hindu populations in India, Nepal, Bali island, etc.

In Hinduism, the administrators, soldiers, police, and some others employed in harder tasks who are known as 'Kshatriyas' can consume meat in a reasonable proportion, besides vegetables in their diet. Hunting, otherwise an inhuman sport, was considered a necessary education for princes, other royalties, governors and men-at-arms in ancient India. Codes of Manu recommend serving meat to the royalties.

On the other hand, if a philosopher or a teacher or a religious leader was to be insensitive to even the slightest pain anywhere in the society, he will do a great disservice to the society. He needs to understand the finer emotions that help create sensitive citizens in the service of the society, who could be lawyers, scientists, preachers, poets, philosophers, etc. The vegetarian food are considered to be a food of choice for those who want to train themselves to become more sensitive. This type of people is classified by Hindus in one word as 'Brahmin', and they are generally die-hard vegetarians. Because Brahmins, who would starve but not take life of other animal, those who are restrained in the use of food, water and air, who would like to take the path of least environment damage, and because it is recommended by the spiritual leaders that the vegetarianism has gained respect among Hindus.

The society has both the types of people and both are needed for healthy growth of any society. Hindus have maintained freedom of diet and in a very clever scheme of social structure, have put the responsibility of protecting vegetarians (philosophers, teachers, poets—Brahmins) from physical assault on non-vegetarians (administrators, kings, soldiers—Kshatriyas), in return for intellectual inputs, scientific discoveries etc, thus making best of both worlds in the quest of individual and societal development. For the persons of non-aggressive disposition, Hindus had developed a non-aggressive fighting technique of defence. They were taught several martial arts that could control the aggressive opponents without harming them. It is said that the defensive martial art, 'Kalaripayattu'[34], still popular in Kerala, was the mother of Kung-Fu and Karate since its transmission into China and Japan via Indian monks who were practising the

34 Kalaripayattu is a very effective defensive martial art. So effective it is that the British rulers of India had to ban its practice and teaching in 1793, fearing the invincibility of the practitioners.

martial-art to protect themselves in the unknown lands, they may have to traverse.

Apart from the above, there are literally hundreds of other reasons to choose either a vegetarian or a non-vegetarian diet. But suffice here to say that Hinduism looks at food as a means of self-development. Eat that which will help you advance in the direction of your choice. The Bhagavad Gita does not place one diet above or below the other diet.

A good answer vegetarians can give when asked as to why are they vegetarians, it could be: 'because we love this world and because we want it to survive longer and because it helps us becoming more sensitive and because we want to take care of you and because it is more natural food for humans'.

Most people think that vegetarianism is central to Hinduism. It is not central, though certainly an important tool for self evolution. The fact, however, is that more than 70 percent of Hindus are non-vegetarians. The recent upsurge in diet-awareness and fad for healthy-eating among Westerners has lent a helping hand in promoting a vegetarian diet. Many Hollywood personalities, fashion gurus, musicians, etc have turned vegetarians.

THREE TYPES OF FOODS

Gita has classified at 17-7,8,9,10 the foods in 3 categories; those foods that would be preferred by 'Satvic' people, those foods that would be chosen by 'Rajasic' people and those foods that would be liked by the 'Tamasic' people.

"The foods that promote longevity, virtue, strength, health, happiness and joy are juicy, smooth, substantial and nutritious. Persons in the mode of goodness (Satva) like such foods; (17-08). Foods that are very bitter, sour, salty, hot, pungent, dry and burning; and cause pain, grief and disease are liked by persons in the mode of passion (Rajas); (17-09). The foods liked by people in the mode of ignorance (Tamas) are stale, having perverted juice, putrid, unnatural, rotten, partly-eaten-and-discarded-by-others, or the foods that are unholy and impure. (17-10)"

The Bhagavad Gita is using a Sanskrit word 'Satvic' to describe that food which is ideal for those seeking God, those who are teachers, authors, philosophers, experts, scientists, advisors, consultants, etc., in a word, for 'Brahmins'. Interestingly, some of the great scientists, philosophers and writers, who were traditionally non-vegetarians, have turned vegetarians of their own choice. This list includes, Mark Twain, Albert Einstein, Leo Tolstoy, Dr. Abdul Kalam, Albert Schweitzer, Charles Darwin, George Bernard Shaw, George Harrison, H G Wells, Immanuel Kant, Leonardo Da Vinci, Ralph Waldo Emerson, Isaac Newton, Spike Milligan, Voltaire, etc. Many Christians believe that even Jesus Christ was a vegetarian although it has not been explicitly stated by him, their conclusion is based partly on his uttering and that of some of the Christian saints.

As Hinduism is all about development, progress and evolution, a man can choose his food, best suited to his desired destination, his occupation and goal. For this reason Hinduism accepts all the various practices and leaves the food decision, veg, non-veg or any other variant to the individual.

VEGETARIANISM IN VARIOUS RELIGIONS

All the religions have discussed both the options and have seen the necessity of both, veg as well as non-veg diet for their followers. As the non-vegetarians are in any case in a very high number, obviously, they do not need preaching eating of non-vegetarian food. The space here is utilized hence to show that each and every religion has attempted to preserve vegetarian diet.

Religious Christians are vegetarians for 40 days each year during the 'Lent', a holy period somewhat akin to Islamic month of Ramadan. 'Lent' starts from 'Ash-Wednesday' and lasts till the end of 'Holy-Thursday' when the 'Good-Friday' begins.

Buddhists have a strong culture of vegetarianism from its inception. The very rise of Buddhism started from their abhorrence towards prevalent animal sacrifice rituals that had become very common place during the period of Siddhartha Gautam Buddha.

Among Hindus, one finds world's largest reservoir of vegetarians. Even those Hindus, who are normally non-vegetarians, will observe 'vegetarian-days' at least once a week or on major religious festivals. This has led to an erroneous understanding that all Hindus are vegetarians. Certainly among Hindus, vegetarians are respected more on account of the fact that most of their teachers, philosophers and priests have been traditionally vegetarians, a practice chosen by them to inculcate sensitivity and sharper insight.

Among the followers of Islam, there is no known scripture-supported tradition of vegetarianism. However, there have been Muslim-vegetarians, throughout its history, chiefly those following Sufi Islam. During debates among co-religionists, the general consensus emerges that meat should be eaten in moderation. In India, in deference to Hindus around them, many Muslims have willingly avoided meat and specially the beef.

Among Zoroastrians, once a year in the 'month of Bahaman', the adherents remain strictly vegetarian. Apart from observing one full month of uninterrupted vegetarianism, devout Zoroastrians observe same penance even once every month on the 'Bahman Roz'. Bahman in the Persian tradition was an angel who governs oxen, sheep and other animals of peaceful disposition. Bahman means 'good thought' and it also means 'nobleman' in Persia, from where the ancient Zoroastrianism emerged. The word Bahman may be a distortion of the word Brahmin, considering common ancestry of Zoroastrianism and Hinduism.

THE HOLY COW

Everyone knows that the cow (and oxen and calves) is considered holy by a Hindu and is, therefore, generally respected and never used as food. Most do not know that besides the cow, there are many other animals that are not eaten by Hindus. This tradition comes from human sensitivity towards more sensible of the animals that are in many ways similar to us.

Uncivilized people were cannibals. A civilized man does not eat another of its own kind, a fellow human. In all the civil societies, either in West, Middle-East or East, man generally does not eat friendly considered animals such as horse, dog, cat or other intelligent animals such as monkey, dolphin etc. All this makes sense, because a man has sensitized himself. He wants to spare the animal who has been his companion, from cruelty of slaughter and placing it on his dining table. An admirable thought.

In Hinduism, they have given a lot more consideration, grown through millennia of continuous contemplation, not available to other cultures of the world, over the issues of life. They found that the animals with five finger-nails on each limb are more intelligent and sensitive, almost possessing same intelligence as a human baby. Their advice, pronounced thousands of years ago, is that humans should not eat 'Panch-Nakhaa' animals. Cat, dog, elephant, monkey, squirrel, mouse, etc come in this group. Slaughtering and eating them would entail deadening of our sensitivity and hence even if the meat of these animals may be very tasteful or nutritious, it is uncivilized to eat them. Amongst rest of the animals that may perhaps be eaten if felt required; an exception has been made for cow and its progeny, being almost a mother to us, supplying us with milk from her udders, just as what our mums have done for us and also because she is elected as the representative from animal world for displaying the love and gratitude of mankind towards all those who are 'speech-less'.

HOLY COW AND NON-UTILITARIAN HINDUISM

There are many explanations for treating cow as holy. Is the main reason being her usefulness? Cow gives milk, ox ploughs the field, and their dung is used as fuel for cooking; and as fertilizer in fields. Dung is used in village-homes for applying on the floor and walls as the predecessor of modern day cement, tiles or paint; being considered to be antiseptic and anti-pests. Cow dung and urine is used as medicines by villagers. Thus it is easy to see why cow is treated as holy and spared from becoming meat by Indians. This is logical and also a common sense. However, this is not the reason for its holy status in the Hinduism.

Because cow is useful is not good enough an explanation why the Vedic sages designated cow to be holy and un-slaughter-able animal. There are other useful animals too; and what if at a given time her usefulness is over? Will her holy status also vanish with it? With advent of tractor, cement, electricity and cooking gas already her usefulness is eroded. And many among us do not even drink milk. Will that erode or end cow's holy status? No, cow is always holy. Every Hindu custom should necessarily have timeless or 'Sanatan' quality, Hinduism being a Sanatan Dharma. Any and every ritual or practice in Hinduism must meet this touchstone.

Holy status is granted to cow because that is required for human development in terms of evolving man to be a better human. It is for a lesson in gratitude and sensitivity.

Child takes his nourishment from mother's milk from the day he is born. Initially he lives exclusively on mother's milk and thereafter on the cow's milk. Nature has produced milk in the udders of cow for nourishing her calves; however we humans have taken her milk, which was not meant for us but was for someone else. Cow's milk became replacement of human's own mother's milk. Cow has thus become mother of human child. Should it not occur to 'human' to thank the cow that has nourished him from his early childhood? Should it not occur to him to say them thank you? And what is the best way to say thank-you, but to protect your mother, your nourishing protector for life time? A man should be able to differentiate, should be able to understand that cow is mother and therefore holy in true sense, even after her milk-producing days are over. Hindus could slaughter and eat up a cow, like anyone else around him but consciously they have chosen not to. They called her 'mother cow', said "thank you" and abstained. Ancient Hindu wisdom says that: "if one spends even a moment 'tolerating and nourishing' me when I am a tiny helpless child, ignorant and demanding, for that person I could well be his/her slave for my whole life time" (meaning I will hold him holy and in high esteem as God).

It is also believed by devout Hindus that cow is divine; it is said to be the seat of God. Some believe that cow becomes human in her next birth and, therefore, she is almost a human. Though cow is venerated from much ancient times before Lord Krishna, many associate cow protection with His love for cows. Lord Krishna was a cow herder as a young boy. Among His several names, 'Gopal' signifies Lord Krishna as the 'Protector and Carer of Cows'. Mahatma Gandhi, whose first name "Mohandas" literally means, "Lord Krishna's servant" said: "When I see a cow, it is not an animal to eat; it is a poem of pity for me and I worship it and I shall defend its worship against the whole world. My religion teaches me that I should, by my personal conduct, instill into the minds of those who might hold different views the conviction that cow-killing is a sin." (*Collected Works of Mahatma Gandhi*, Vol. XXV).

The voluntary sacrificing of the temptation to eat beef, out of respect and just to say 'thank-you' is a great achievement in terms of human evolution and self-control. In that sense, it stands out in stark contrast to the pork-abstinence of Muslims, which is not out of respect or even sympathy for animal, they do it because they consider pig as 'unclean' and therefore a no-no.

Knowledgeable Hindu, hungry and even in the dire need of food would not think of beef. He is taught restraint, a restraint with respect, a restraint without complaint. As the protection of cows is meant for self-development of humans, in that sense the cow protection is more than a mere religious rule. Mahatma Gandhi said: "Cow protection is the gift of Hinduism to the world"- (Mahatma, Ed. D.G. Tendulkar, Vol. 2, 2nd Ed., 1960). He said: "Cow protection means protection of the weak, the helpless, the dumb and the deaf." (*Collected Works of Mahatma Gandhi*, Vol. XXVI).

In deference to sentiments of Hindus and the wishes of Mahatma Gandhi, even to this day, slaughter of cows and its progeny is banned in most of India (with an exception of Hindu-depleted states).[35] In India, the cows are cared even after their milk-giving days are over. Instead of consigning them to the slaughter houses, they are rested, fed and paid medical attention till their natural death by literally thousands of NGOs, supported by ordinary Hindus from their private incomes.

Footwears of Mahatma Gandhi were not made from skin of a butchered animal but an animal that died naturally. To remember his legacy even today Indian government is supporting[36] cottage-industry across the country and its shops sell the footwears made from skins of un-slaughtered, naturally dead animals.

---

35 Hindu depleted states are: Jammu and Kashmir, Nagaland, Tripura, Meghalaya and Mizoram.

36 Legacy of Mahatma Gandhi is kept alive by 'Khadi and Village Industries Commission'.

HOLY COW IN OTHER RELIGIONS AND CULTURES

Most cultures have in some or other way acknowledged their gratefulness towards cow. Among the ancients, the cow worship had been common in India, among Germanic tribes of Europe and among Vikings of northern Europe. Zoroastrians of ancient Persia have rituals involving worshipping spotless white calf even now. In the book of Exodus, Bible refers to the sacred golden calf.

The term "holy cow" has found its way in English and American expressions under the influence of the practice that was witnessed by colonial powers among Hindus where killing of a cow gave stigma to a person, comparable to murdering a pious Brahmin, the ultimate crime.

Gender Bias in Hinduism, Male-Female, and the 'Third Kind'[37]

All the main-stream religions of the world have disappointed the feminists to more or less degrees, and certainly abhorred those not classified as either male or female, the 'Third kind', the transvestites.

Gods, God's messengers and Prophets have always been Males in religions other than Hinduism. Vedas unequivocally state that the God is both male and female and have symbolically shown Lord Shiv having both the aspects in his well known form as 'Ardha Nari-Nateshwar' (Half-Man-Half-Women, Shiv; the Patron-God of Artists).

Hinduism even freely allows a place for 'the third gender-'third-kind' or those having indeterminable gender. One of the

37 'Third Kind' are those born naturally with confusing gender or confusing characteristic, more appropriately described as trans-gender or tranvestites. 'Third Kind' is loosely translated in English as 'Eunuch', who are most often castrated males for service in the harems.

commanders of the Mahabharat War, Shikhandi[38] had a place among the senior officers in the army. Even today in India, the 'third kinds' have their own societies, own deities, own way of worship[39] and customs. Indeed, the 'third-kinds' do not escape discrimination, an outcome of the natural intrigue surrounding them; fostered by society, but never by the Hinduism.

The Bhagavad Gita is for everyone in the mankind, therefore, obviously includes women. In its entire text, nowhere is the woman mentioned separately for either praise or for vilification. The word 'women' appears thrice in the Gita; at 1-41, 9-32 and at 10-34. All three references affirm importance and esteem of women. Verse 1-41 is spoken by Arjun, who is concerned about women facing the consequences of aftermath of the war. Rest two verses are spoken by Lord Krishna. At 9-32, He emphasizes 'women' lest anyone forget them among the common term 'everyone' when Lord Krishna says that everyone who has loving devotion towards God can attain Supreme Abode (Liberation). Let alone the devout sages, but businessmen (vaishya), servicemen (shudra), women and even a sinner can reach the liberation by loving devotion to God. And in 10-34, Lord Krishna lists the qualities of fame, prosperity, speech, memory, intellect, resolve, and forgiveness that are resident in the women by calling these qualities as His Divine manifestations among women.

Women are so important in the life of a Hindu that hardly any Hindu God or sage is without a wife. A wife that is not a mere 'show-piece' or an 'assistant' standing beside her spouse but she has her own independent role or an individual standing. Goddess Lakshmi, wife of Lord Vishnu, is controlling Goddess of wealth. Goddess Saraswati, the Goddess of Knowledge,

---

38 Shikhandi was said to have been born a girl but raised like a boy. More commonly he is described as a eunuch, although an object of ridicule, Shikhandi was appreciated for his valour.

39 Present day 'third kinds' are known as 'Hijaras' in India and they worship Goddess Yellammma.

is fiercely independent and does not even accept marrying any man, lest it compromise her intellectual freedom, held so paramount in Hinduism. Hinduism is a synonym for intellectual freedom. Story of Goddess Saraswati goes to say how male-supremacy is not a core idea in the Hinduism.

No Hindu religious ceremony can be completed without wife[40]. Manu-Smruti (The law book of Hindus) declares at verse 56 of Chapter 3, that: "Where women are respected, the Gods would be happy and if women are not respected, the rituals and ceremonies would prove to be useless". In the next verses, 57-58-59 it adds: "If women are unhappy, those who cause her unhappiness will be destroyed along with their clan and if women are happy, their house and their clan, both would prosper. Those who want to be happy should keep women happy". During the religious ceremonies, it is only the wife who provides fire for the start of the rituals and in the end, the sacrament (sacrificial objects). Without a wife, a religious ceremony thus can neither start nor end. Husband and wife are always meant to be together, summed up in the wedding vows as together in everything, 'Dharmech, Kamech, Arthech, Mokshech' (Translated, we are together in every activity, be it for fulfilling duty, be it for pleasure, be it for earning or be it for attaining Moksha, Nirvan, Liberation). The word used for sex in the Sanskrit language is very significant in showing the status of women. The word is 'Sambhog' meaning 'equal-enjoyment' for both. Wife is known as 'Ardhangana', meaning she forms 50 percent of the body of husband; which goes to say that without

40 For a married person, it is absolutely mandatory in Hinduism that the religious ceremonies such as Yajna have to be performed as a couple. Husband alone cannot perform any Yajna ceremony. Even the God is not exempt from this rule. In a classical case noted by Sage Valmiki in his epic poetry Ramayana', Lord Rama was not allowed to perform Yajna without his wife Sita. In her physical absence, the Yajna-authority (the person who preside the ceremony) compelled Lord Rama to keep a statue of Sita as a commitment of Lord Rama towards Sita while performing the Yajna ceremony.

the wife, a husband is just 'half' or 'incomplete'. She is also known as a 'Saha-Dharma-Charini' (One who always walks together in the performance of duties, the 'Dharma').

Mother, (and indeed father too), have a status of God for their children and are treated with respect reserved for Gods.[41]

Women have the freedom to choose their husband from the time immemorial. No other culture of the world has seen an elaborate 'Swayamvar' (translated, Swayamvar means 'a ceremonial occasion where the bride herself chooses for her a husband') institution as was present in India. Lord Rama was chosen among hundreds of aspiring grooms by Sita. Swayamvars were held by the girl's parents when the girl decides to marry. Swayamvar-law states that the decision of the girl is incontestable. Anyone disputing the girl's decision automatically became enemy and has to face fight with all the aspiring grooms and the parents of the bride.

Laws in India, just as in Western countries do allow for legal divorce, however, traditional Hinduism does not allow divorce; it is incumbent upon the husband to ensure smooth marriage for life; no matter what difficulty. The marriage is for life. Manu-Smruti sees in a wife a role of an empress. It asks the new bride to become (worthy of being) 'like a commanding empress' of the household, and rule the house.

It is an irony that the above stated lofty outlook for women in Hinduism is not what one finds in the Hindu society today. During the dark period of invasions and foreign occupation, the independence of women was curtailed. They could not venture out for the fear of being kidnapped by invaders. They were forced to veil themselves on lines of females of Muslim rulers. Music, dancing and schooling were frowned upon and even banned from time to time. Under their tyranny of more than a thousand years, the societal behaviour had to be modified

41 "Matru Devo Bhava, Pitru Devo Bhava" (Mother becomes my God, Father becomes my God).

by Hindus for their survival. The style of the royals became fashionable. Hindus adopted their style, their language, and their customs and superimposed them on their own traditions. This resulted in Hindu women facing the same fate as Muslim women. However, different groups among Hindus have treated their women differently, thereby Hindu women still had chance to overcome oppressions on them when the influence of Muslim kings faded. However, the dark period of tyrannical rule did take its toll. Today although many women are CEOs, Government Ministers, senior bureaucrats, they generally have a secondary importance among traditional Hindu households. They are either naturally self satisfied in the supportive role in preference to the principal role, or are forced into accepting a supportive secondary role due to peer pressures or circumstances. In India Hindu women, however, still gets more freedom than their counterparts in Islamic world and have better safety nets and family support than their Western counterparts. In the best scenarios, women have held highest political positions, as Mrs. Indira Gandhi had, and in the worst scenarios, widows have been burnt alive as 'Sati', female foetuses have been aborted and brides have been burnt if came without sufficient dowry, far from the lofty ideals of the Vedas.

Fortunately, the ingenuity of the Hindu society created many reformers, who took up the cause of women and helped them live a life of dignity, notably, Raja-Rammohun Roy, Mahatma Gandhi and Maharishi Karve. It must also be noted however that the repression and misery faced by women was not a universal fact throughout the country. There were thousands of instances even during the dark millennium, indicating educated, brilliant women leaders.

Even under the worst situation, Hindus as a society or as a religion never treated their women as a saleable commodity, as an object, as a slave. Hinduism has no place for 'Muta', the 'temporary marriage' system practised among the Muslims though not approved by Islam in normal conditions, nor is considered 'a devil's gateway' or 'the first corrupter of Divine Law' as stated in the Christian texts. The testimony in a court of law by a woman in Hinduism is not invalid or half-valued as is the case of woman's testimony in Sharia[42]. At no stage in its long history, has Hinduism asked their women to veil or double veil (Old Testament asks women to double veil in public).

Hindu society is blessed with thousands of women of achievements from ancient times until today. Hindu texts have described various distinguished women, some sages, some brave warriors, some diplomats, some emissaries, some spies and many who have been serious advisors to their mighty husbands.

Even today what we find it as rather rare in the world, except in India that a woman can occupy high chairs of Prime Ministers, Chief Ministers and Presidents. Indian women had voting power well before Blacks acquired it in America. Today India has women as its President[43]. The Indian Constitution provides to women all the powers as men. Remember, all these, despite the sad fact that the colonizers and conquerors of India had severely damaged the ancient social structures.

Slavery

It is significant that in the Indian history one will hardly find 'slavery' akin to what one finds in the history of Middle-East, Africa, Europe or Americas. For this, perhaps the credit goes to the Hindu concept that every human is divine and, therefore, the human body cannot be bought. The body even does not belong to the soul that is in an individual. In other words, my body does not even belong to me, how can I sell or purchase it? And how it could be purchased by anyone and controlled by anyone? This is precisely the logic for outlawing the murder as well as suicide. When one does not own one's body, what right one has to destroy it?

---

42 Sharia is the Islamic Law, held compulsory in many Islamic countries.

43 President of India Mrs. Pratibha Patil

History of slavery practice of Europe and America is blood-curdling. Slave catching, transporting, selling at auctions and how they were treated are a blot on the humanity. Slaves were rounded up by 'civilized' armies of Egypt, Greece and Rome during the ancient times. In the later times, Turks and Muslim invaders took slaves from the territories that they ran over. In modern times Europeans took slaves from Africa, South America and Central America for selling in the 'new-territories', the North America.

Until the savage arrival of foreign conquerors, India had not seen anything like slavery in their long history of thousands of years. However, Alexander, Taimur, Nadir and scores of others took, not thousands but literally millons of Indian men, women and children as slaves over last two thousand years. These slaves have by now assimilated in the foreign lands and are not so visible, one exception being the Gypsies, still roaming Europe.

The Caste-System (The Varna-Ashram-Dharma)

Caste system is present in every society by one or the other name or namelessly. Hermann Hesse (1877-1962), who won his Nobel Prize for Literature for his path-breaking book: 'The Glass Bead Game', this book explains nothing else but the European form of 'Varna-Ashram-Dharma'. Hermann applied the insight he obtained while reading Hindu literature and especially a story from the Vishnu Purana[44]. He noticed that while Indians had given the names to the castes and done the in-depth classification, Europeans were not advanced enough to classify the already existing and working but invisible caste system in Western countries. From the ancient times in India, they had classified professions into four broad categories and made rules that primed every member of the society in his own profession.

44 One of the principal Puranas.

1. Studying and teaching
2. Protecting
3. Trading and farming
4. Serving

In the Bhagavad Gita, at 4-13, Lord Krishna says with His own mouth that: "I created the four divisions of human society based on aptitude and vocation."

Caste Differences, Real and Unreal

For Hindus, the caste system and caste-based discrimination has been a major issue and an embarrassment. It is said to be unjust system that creates 'high' and 'low' classification of people by virtue of their birth. It is said that in this system a person from 'high' caste is treated with higher priority than a 'low' caste individual even if the former is an idiot and the later is highly educated, or even rich. Also, the system seems to put the 'low'caste people at societal disadvantage that he remains poor, his opportunities are snatched and he lives a life of a reject. Brahmins are said to be at the top of the caste-ladder with the Shudras being the lowest. Some who are lower than the lowest, the Dalits, who are outcastes and are untouchables. What a sad commentary. Why would Lord Krishna claim His ownership on this, clearly an unjust caste system in the Gita? It, therefore, becomes an interesting subject to investigate in more depth.

Even for those who would appreciate everything in the Bhagavad Gita and in general would agree to Hindu philosophy, would find it hard to subscribe to the caste system, described universally as bane of Hinduism. In the otherwise a brilliant philosophy, caste-system stands out like a sore thumb.

Ninety nine percent of evangelists successfully use the 'caste card' as their trump-card in their effort of denouncing Hinduism and for converting Hindus into Christianity or Islam. Mahatma Gandhi was so sick and tired of hearing this rhetoric from every Tom, Dick and Harry that he once said of those writers, speakers and journalist who talk nothing else about Hinduism except the caste-system are like 'Gutter-Inspectors'. They come to India and become an 'expert' in a few days time they stay here, and like an authority they talk about untouchability and caste-discrimination and start giving sermons. (Instead of studying it first, and also looking at other grand ideas of Indian culture that has produced so many wonderful things that are sadly absent among the critics.) They, as what gutter inspectors do, only examine the gutter and give its report, important though for menders of gutters, should not be allowed to hijack discussion on Hinduism and of India on this one aspect alone. In truth, the caste system is not properly studied by most including the so-called champions of Hinduism. It has many essential life-supporting and human development facets.

In the persent context, it is a fact that the holy stream that was the Varna-Ashram-Dharma (the caste system) has become polluted, deserving its description as gutter by the Mahatma. Serious readers will pause and pursue more investigation; when considering ills of caste-system and trying to throw it off. Are we throwing the baby with the bath-tub? Are there any advantages to accrue from the Varna-Ashram-Dharma? Does it have any merit at all?

BRAHMIN, CASTE THAT STUDY AND TEACH

The class of people, who study and teach in the spirit of service to God, are known as 'Brahmins'. Their role in the society was to teach at schools and universities, provide advice when required by anybody, without discrimination including to the rulers, observe austerities and perform spiritual rituals. In the pursuit of their vocation of excelling in various knowledges, they had to spend their life mainly in studies and could ill-afford time spent on luxuries. They led a highly disciplined and frugal life, devoid of even minimal luxury. A Brahmin is expected to sleep not more than 6 hours a day, who sleeps on hard floor and uses minimum clothes. Apart from being a vegetarian, he would observe several fasts and challenge his body and mind to remain uncorrupted. Fiercely independent minded Brahmin community would generally remain independent and would not accept salary from anyone, lest he has to sway his opinion in the employer's favour. Most advisors to the rulers were on honorary service and thereby could give their opinions without fear or favour.

Brahmin's code of conduct was severest. (It is same as a lawyer or a policeman, who is liable for harsher punishment than others in today's courts, being knowledgeable yet defying rules). Members of this community if convicted of any wrong doing were liable to severest punishment[45]. Even a small crime was considered a big crime and attracted heavy penalty. In the event, ruler does not punish him; a conscientious Brahmin would take self-punishment. There are documented cases when he has inflicted self–punishment or has gone to ruler begging him for the penalty.

Consequent to his way of life, Brahmin, was neither wealthy nor could exercise any political power. Yet in terms of respect enjoyed, no other class could rival. Even the ruler would bow to him. As a state advisor he received immunity from punishment for speaking his mind out even to the rulers. This class, though poverty ridden, kept the conscience of the community. This class could not be corrupted and was always ready for sacrifices in favour of truth. His code of conduct tells him to always give an unbiased advice to anyone seeking it, even to an adversary.

During the outside aggression and occupation of India by foreigners, it was this class that faced the worst brunt, owing

45 Manu-Smruti Chapter 8, Verse 336 States: "In a case where a common man would be fined one unit, the King will be fined 1000, that is the established rule. For theft, the penalty on a Shudra is 8 times the value of the object stolen, on a Vaishya 16, on a Kshatriya 32 times, and on a Brahmin 64 times, or 100 times or even 132 times, since he knows the nature of the offence."

to their refusal to kneel down to the power. Such defiance, by a whole group, disregarding prospect of death, was not seen by invaders anywhere else in the world. They could not understand how the entire group, a group that had no way to defend, had no weapons, had no financial support, was ready to die but not succumb. The invaders were puzzled and fearing revolt simply killed them. First documented massacre of Brahmins took place during Alexander's invasion. First massacre by Muslim invaders happened when Daher, the last Hindu King of Sindh, was defeated by Turks.

After having settled down in India, and having secured their borders and establishing administration, Muslim invaders and British rulers of India did use Brahmins owing to their intellectual brilliance, though cautiously as they were suspicious of them and never gave them any position of influence or any un-supervised position.

In Sanskrit, the word 'Brahmin' would mean those who are engaged in the work of the 'Brahm' (the God). To learn and teach is considered the work one must do for God and thereby take society upwards on the evolutionary path. To learn is to evolve. Most advisors, experts of every discipline and priests, were generally from this class. In the Gita, at 18-42, Lord Krishna says: "The natural activity-karma-profession-duty of a 'Brahmin' is to work for acquiring serenity, self control, austerity, purity, patience, honesty, knowledge, transcendental knowledge, transcendental experience, and belief in God".

KSHATRIYA, CASTE THAT PROTECTS LIFE AND PROPERTY, UPHOLDS JUSTICE

In Sanskrit language, Kshatriya means, 'those who protect'. Thus the class of people that protects, is called 'Kshatriya'. Rulers, civil administrators, army and police personnel can be said to be having Kshatriya traits. They are Kshatriyas if they do their job with an attitude of service to God. The Gita, at 18-43, describes "Heroism, vigor, firmness, dexterity, not fleeing from battle, charity and leadership are the natural activity-karma-profession-duty of 'Kshatriya."

However, in terms of their duty to state, they followed though a strict codes of conduct; was much liberal than meant for Brahmins. They would be subject to harsh punishment if found violating the laws. The exception is made for the ruler. The 'king can do no wrong' was stated in different words by ascribing a status of divinity to the kings. Except the king, rests of the Kshatriyas were under normal rules. Even this day in most countries, their presidents and prime ministers and the ruling chiefs, such as kings and sheikhs have constitutional immunity (or in some cases, some degree of protection) from prosecution.

Code of conduct of Kshatriya does not allow him to discriminate between people he is required to protect. Every member of the society has to be protected by him; if necessary even by happily laying his life for him. He is compelled by his code of conduct to provide shelter and refuge to anyone seeking it, including to a surrendering enemy. History has not witnessed any massacre of the surrendered enemy by a Hindu ruler, ever. Members of this community were thought to be physically strong, disciplined, brave, unafraid of death, and when challenged, would never shy away from fight. They were well rewarded by the rulers and hence generally were moderately rich and enjoyed the luxuries and influence that go with power. Obviously, a class appeased by all, except Brahmins, who will not succumb even to the most powerful.

It is very interesting to note that almost all the incarnations of God are born Kshatriya (and hardly any Brahmin). The creator of the Bhagavad Gita, Lord Krishna, the hero of Ramayana, Lord Rama, the latest incarnation, Lord Gautam Buddha, all were born Kshatriyas. Even the sage-king, the law giver, Manu, was a Kshatriya.

VAISHYA, CASTE OF TRADERS AND FARMERS

The business and farming class is known as 'Vaishya' if their activity is conducted in the spirit of service to God. They are generators of wealth. They are predisposed to business tactics and foresight. At 18-44, the Gita states: "Cultivation, cattle rearing, business, trade, finance, and industry are the natural activity-karma-profession-duty of the Vaishya."

They feed and nourish society and hence the word "Vaishya', meaning in Sanskrit: 'those who feed and nourish and who is welcome in any home'. Trade and business have no boundaries and no discrimination. True free-trade.

Vaishyas followed a much more liberalized living code, indulged in lavish living, and were reasonably educated to be able to become effective business persons. Vaishyas are naturally a rich community as compared to Brahmins and Kshatriyas. In times of crisis, they are known to have lent money even to the kings.

In case of criminal offences, they were punished but not as severely as were punished Brahmins for an identical offence.

SHUDRA, CASTE OF SERVICE PROVIDERS

At 18-44, Gita states: "Serving others is the natural activity-karma-profession-duty of 'Shudra'". The service providers' class was the most prosperous class of all four classes. Without a Brahmin, world can survive, without a Kshatriya, the world can survive perhaps with some disorder, even without a trader, perhaps one can survive but not even a day without the skilled workers, the Shudras. They are contractors, builders, carpenters, plumbers, electricians, engineers, blacksmiths, goldsmiths, sailors, doctors, surgeons, etc of the world. Their profession lent themselves to become indispensable and lead more prosperous life, as they could demand their fees.

It is thought that, temperamentally, Shudras are sentimental, are easily excitable and they are straight thinkers.

The Sanskrit meaning of Shudra is 'those with a sympathetic heart'. Their heart bleeds to see a man in pain and they are happy to see a happy man. Shudras worked independently and they provided the services in the spirit of 'service to God'.

As is the case with most rich and affluent, these people as a class are more into luxury and less into asceticism. Naturally, they are more into extravaganza and less into puritan abstinence. Law was most lenient with this class as they were not expected really to be able to discern what their obligations were to the community in general. Though they did attend the trade-schools, very rarely did they go to institutions of higher education, meaning, live-in Gurukul Ashram Schools, equivalent to the present-day universities, where the deeper knowledge of art of life was imparted.

Caste-system: Trade License?

Caste system can be somewhat compared to present-day system of trade licensing wherein the profession of the establishment is defined by the concerned government authority. One is allowed to officially carry out the business that is specified on the license. For every new activity, another license and/or amendment are required. For instance, a goldsmith cannot practise business of home-construction and vice versa. During ancient times, the formal license was although not existing, the person was required to stick to his father's profession and never to change that profession. To change the profession without state permission was a punishable crime. Change of profession of a person tantamounts to change of his caste, a change permissible only with Ruler's explicit permission. There are extremely rare examples in the history when the changes were allowed. This system guaranteed professional skill, eliminated unfair rat-race competition, and provided life-long professional protection. However, it is also open to critics from time immemorial that it takes away the freedom to choose the profession, indeed a truth; but provides stability to society, mental-peace and freedom within one's own profession, in which he is naturally most efficient. This practice ensured that the caste system remained insulated from any corruption from rich and powerful. Till date caste-system has not been corrupted in the sense that even a wealthy man or a brainy man cannot call his caste differently; even a king has to belong to the caste he is born into.

Caste-System: Profession-based but in Effect Birth-based

At 18-41, Lord Krishna clearly states: "O Arjun, the activities (karma, work, profession) of 'Brahmin', 'Kshatriya', 'Vaishya' and 'Shudras' has been classified based on the qualities inherent to people's nature and their make up." Thus we know that the origin of the Vedic caste system was based on profession of the individual. However, to adopt a system based on the profession would mean that a man first gets into the profession and then based on his profession, his caste be determined. When that man gets his child, what training will he impart to him? Is it feasible to first evaluate his leanings and then train him for a particular profession? Yes that is what we do today. We give general education to a child in a school for 10-12 years and then he takes up a particular syllabus in university and gets his degree. Even armed with a degree, he is not yet sure as to if he will get a job, and what kind of job will he get. And even after getting the job, he needs further training in that particular activity of his employer. Even after working several years, he still has the threat of dismissal, sacking and relocating. A man is always on tenterhooks, always unsure and worried for his bread. A man needs 15-20 years of education to earn his bread. And if he does not get a job, he starves, begs, steals or lives on the handouts of government or charity. Our current society has made it harder for humans to earn their own bread than even a dog, who earns it without ever going to a class. If the man gets a job, he must retain it at any cost, even if that means accepting insults, doing thing that he would not like to do and, the worst still, act on the whims and fancies of his boss. Belittling his great potential a man is reduced into meek, 'yes-man', jealous, and perpetually worried person. And he would still let his child undergo the same grind that he has passed through. He has no escape, what else can he do in the current system?

When a child is born in a family, he starts to learn from day one. He picks up a wealth of knowledge on a day-to-day basis from the world around him from the childhood. This knowledge is known in Sanskrit as 'Sanskar'. Sanskar is different from conscious education. It is stored in the unconscious brain and keeps a strong lifelong, indelible presence. The activities of the parents are stored in the child's mind. Moreover, genetic researchers have noted that parents' many characteristics are inherited by the child. The believers in the rebirth know that the particular child has chosen to be born in that family because he already has some skills of his parents that he can further hone while in that family. He is thus better predisposed to the profession of the parents. Vedic philosophers chose to capitalize on his existing knowledge-base of the individual instead of wasting it away.

The child's training has already begun from his birth much before parents even think about teaching their child. If parents let the child participate in their profession, he will acquire skills for that profession much faster. He learns parent's vocation easily and naturally. He becomes familiar with professional secrets and skills. He ultimately becomes even better at the profession than his parents. Armed with profession in his hand he is independent, he does not have to degrade himself, below the life of that dog, who wags his tail at anybody who so much as just shows him a piece of bread.

His entire resource base is negated when a child chooses a profession different from his parents. Vedic philosophers, therefore, decided to impart to the child the training of profession of his parents. Thus automatically, parents' profession became child's profession in the Vedic caste system. And the profession-based system automatically became effectively a 'birth-based' system. A Brahmin's child was a Brahmin, a Kshatriya child a Kshatriya, Vaishya's Vaishya and Shudra's Shudra. Birth of a child sealed his profession. Every individual knew from beginning as to what his profession would be and that his job was ensured with almost same earning potential as any other activity. It was recognized that a plumber or a surgeon both required almost same amount of food and other basic necessities. Also that he was a free man; not a paid servant at the whim and fancy of his employer and that his services were always required, lent him self-esteem and recognition in the society. Vedic caste-system was meant for healthy regulation of day-to-day life, with a noble view of letting everyone have a fair chance of 'human development' by remaining away from the rat-race and be able to spend some time for self-development. Caste system is, therefore, known as a 'duty'; 'dharma', technically known as the 'Varna-Ashram-Dharma.'

Caste-System Purpose: Long-term Stability in a Society

'Survival of the fittest' is the law. Our business and political models work on this law of the jungle. We are civilized, we do not live in jungle anymore but our slogan remains 'perform or perish'. We are leading our lives today, fully knowing that no one can remain fit for the whole life. We dread the day when we would be redundant. The Vedic sages thought of a society where we fit the individual to survive and prosper, with every member of society providing a useful service, whatever is his profession or his age.

Today our relationships have a stink of exploitation. Our relationships are marked by exploitation of the needy. Today's trade-model teaches us to sell at maximum feasible price and buy at minimum possible price. So we are all out to exploit each other. We inherently do not like to be exploited but see no harm in exploiting others. However, at the end of the day we are exploited by possessor of that commodity that we do not have but want. A lawyer will exploit a doctor and vice versa.

Uncertainty of earning the wages is a source of tension even in the advance societies of the world. Sounding almost like Marxists but with Vedic input, the thinkers of Vedas had a spiritual yet logical and earthy practical scheme. They knew, 'the labour of an individual cannot be measured. All labour is invaluable. It is the outcome of the God given basic abilities'. Therefore, the work done was considered worship and was not priced. However, as a practical way of life in a society, all services rendered were almost uniformly paid because we all humans need basically almost the same or similar things for living; bread, clothes and shelter. In today's world, a plumber earns Dollars 10 per hour and a surgeon earns Dollars 1000 per hour although surgeon's stomach is not hundred times bigger, if at all it would be smaller.

Today most of us have reduced ourselves into a mere wage earner. A man hankering to find a master to whom he would serve. He has a constant worry of finding a job. He does everything to qualify to get the employment, to look good for the job, to look better-equipped than other candidate, to outsmart his fellow human.

A man emerging from a college is unsure what job will he find. Even after getting the job, sometimes he does not understand why he is paid so little for so much work put in by him and why the other gets a lot more money for hardly any work, apparently it is not only the work. And a fine craftsman gets fired when the employer finds that his business is not profitable or that he wants to close his business in favour of other more lucrative business; thereby leaving the master craftsman in lurch, unemployed, income-deprived or necessitating learning new crafts for new employer in his advancing years, wasting already learnt skills.

In this spider web of earning livelihood, a man is constantly on the run, trying to dodge the stalking spider. In his constant quest for earning wage, he is focused on honing his abilities to get a job and retain it at any cost. He has no time for anybody in the world. He has no time to even understand who he is; to see what jewel that he is, crafted by the Master Craftsman that God is. He has no time to brood over his purpose in the life. His is the monumental story of Solomon Grundy, who was born on Monday till he is buried on Sunday. He has no time to see if he is exploiting others, is he getting exploited by others, is he taking more from nature without giving back to nature. It is just he, himself and his things and his rights.

Does he have a way out of this sap-draining system? Is there any other better system? Yes, there is; at least there was one, until contaminated and now nearly destroyed, Vedic Varna-Ashram-System.

In the Vedic caste system, it was essential element that every individual had to be independent. To be fixed at a periodical wage in service of someone was considered to be an unfortunate, last resort, that would not ultimately give a person any mental satisfaction. Practitioner of every trade would work till he has earned enough for the day and the balance time would be spent on his family, on recreation and for his own self-development, assured fully that he will not have to face any unfair competition. This was the typical atmosphere in a society during the Vedic times. Ancient stories are replete with examples of people lamenting for being in servitude of nobles or kings. This was especially true for Brahmins. In Mahabharat, Kaurav's archery-and-warfare teacher Guru Drona laments his acceptance of job to become a paid royal teacher. He blames his acceptance of paid job citing his poverty.

The Varna-Ashram-Dharma is based on a charter of duties, whereas today we are working on the charter of rights. It is fashionable to demand rights. There are well-defined rules concerning everyone's rights. On the other hand, there are no rules regarding duties.

Consider with open mind, has any philosopher of the world, from ancient Greece to modern Europe and America, from Aristotle to Karl Marx, if there has been any society that worked without charter of rights but only on the charter of duties like what was present in India in the form of Varna-Ashram-Dharma? A society that survived thousands of years, the society that created a vibrant, non-oppressive benevolent culture, a society that created one of the most perfect languages (Sanskrit) of the world, extensive literature, mathematics, trigonometry, astronomy, the list is endless. All became possible because the caste system freed people to have the precious time. It freed people's minds from existential worries.

Vedic caste system does need anyone to defend it. It stands out on its own merit. It has survived over thousands of years and has proven to have worked well. It has even till today remained alive, despite Herculean efforts of Hindu reformists and governments and denouncement by every section of the society. It makes an interesting study to find reasons, why this system still survives? From where does it get its oxygen?

Also, a social analyst will note that the above system effectively ensured that each caste had a distinct, one specific unique strength, whose livelihood will never be challenged and still he will have to decidedly depend on other members of society for other skills, as he himself will not have the skill of other. A social scientist will realize the value of this system. This system will keep, in effect, each one healthily interdependent so that the entire society lives in harmony with comfortable feel of belonging and being needed. Inherently, it was a non-exploitative society that ensured steady income for everyone and warmth of being wanted. The rich did not become richer and the poor did not become poorer.

Consider also the following: The knowledge-oriented person (Brahmin) will have limited wealth, and strength; the strength-oriented person (Kshatriya) will have limited knowledge and wealth; the wealth-oriented person (Vaishya) will have limited knowledge and strength; and the skill-oriented person (Shudra) will have limited knowledge and strength yet none can be ignored and none can live without the other. Thus, each caste depends for survival on all the rest of the castes, ensuring a mutually cooperative interdependence.

Also, consider one more aspect: A society that permits any one of its member to possess more than two attributes, invites eventual self destruction of that society. Consider the exploitative power of a person, who has two attributes—the wealth and knowledge—such as owners of Microsofts and IBMs, accumulating enormous wealth, monopolizing and exploiting rest of the world. The other combination, the wealth and power can create Opecs and Halliburtons. The third combination, the knowledge and power can create cartels of G8 countries, the atomic powers, NSG, or leagues of space-powers who would frighten and extract pound of flesh from the rest. The auto-pilot system created by Vedic sages never allowed these three (Knowledge-Strength-Wealth) or any two of these powers to be monopolized by any one individual or one particular caste, thus eliminating danger to the world of terrible exploitative power.

We are all aware of the exploitative powers of these combinations. No one wants to be negatively affected by Microsofts, IBMs, OPECs, Halliburtons, etc. but no one has any vaccine against their exploitative power. Some governments have tried but have not been effective. However, these are only commercial companies, perhaps they can be controlled but now think of a possibility of what can happen if one possesses all the three attributes, the triple-some exploitative power. The heads of capitalist countries, heads of communist countries, heads of fascist countries have at their finger tips, enormous brain power, huge muscle power and unprecedented financial power drawn from their nations. Think of their exploitative powers. The deadly equation. There is no way of telling what he will not do; a man can degenerate into a vicious demon.

In the Vedic times, kings were not controlling brains or finances; they had to only administer using the tax money. And the tax money was to come from people, in a manner, "as if a bee sucks the nectar from a flower"; not harming the flower but pollinating it and returning its favour with higher dividends.

Brahmins, though poor and devoid of any political power, were seen as 'high' due to their knowledge and selfless service and so also Kshatriyas were considered 'high' on account of their need being felt by people in the times of life-threatening crisis. Business community, Vaishyas would automatically command respect because they are provider of materials, and service providing Shudras would be in demand for providing skills of all kinds. Thus every section of the society was felt needed and so was respected.

Apart from the profession-related angle to the caste-system, the Varna-Ashram-Dharma has a special appeal among genetic scientists and genographists due to its fall-out in terms of 'planned-human-breeding'. It was a successful experiment in human breeding for developing desirable traits. Industry is spending millions on animal breeding for obtaining species with specific select qualities. However, owing to ethical reasons breeding research on human is limited in the modern world. In-built genetic engineering of Hindu caste-system can help understanding how till date, certain skills and characteristics are retained in the families for generations. Marriages were almost always confined to the same caste. Due to this discipline, even today if one was to check the caste profile of Hindu employees anywhere in the world, you will not be disappointed. Even today you will find their job choices to be predictable. With many cross-marriages now, the boundries are blurring but still visible.

Those who can foresee progress of a society for next thousand years will understand the value of caste system of Vedas. Boldly and unequivocally, Lord Krishna has accepted His authorship of caste-system. As for us, who criticize the caste-system do not even know in what sort of society will our next generation would live in.

The Vedic caste system worked well for thousands of years. As everything corrupts, this great system also got corrupted for some reasons, analyzed below and became so distorted that the original system is not recognizable in what is found today.

Present-day Distortion in the Caste System

Work-culture today is completely different from what was during the Vedic times. Today the work is paid and is based on equation of exploitative abilities. The nurses in a hospital are paid a certain wage but if their shortages are experienced due to their demand elsewhere, the same nurses would be paid more, even double for the same work. The wage is not paid commensurate with work but is paid commensurate with relative exploitative powers of employee and employer. The same is true for price of a product; it is determined by the exploitative powers of customer and supplier. Today most people are employees serving a master. Today the main objective is to earn as much money as possible, because success is measured by money. Brahmins, Kshatriyas and Vaishyas; all have taken up jobs of the Shudras, leaving Shudras marginalized and poor over period of time.

Although, the ancient work culture based on Varna-Ashram-Dharma is not being practised, the Varna-Ashram-

Dharma wedding[46] practices are still more or less being followed. Generally weddings are performed within the same caste (but in a different Gotra[47]). A Brahmin boy would generally marry a Brahmin girl and a Vaishya boy to a Vaishya girl, etc. This ensured genetically preserved characteristics and distinct lineages based on the caste. Even to this date those characteristics are visible and more or less identifiable from the family names of Hindus.

With increased urbanization and much more intermingling of people of different castes, these days, many marriages are taking place outside their castes, adding to existing distortions.

With neither caste performing their roles, yet having physical presence of the castes, the present-day caste system has automatically reduced to just a hierarchical system where Brahmins, Kshatriyas and Vaishyas are considered 'higher castes', and Shudras the lower caste. This is not justified by the scriptures and runs in contradiction to the aims and objectives of the Vedic Varna-Ashram system. In addition, at some point in time in the history, the so-called 'untouchables' have also crept in, in a complete antithesis to the Vedic Hindu philosophy. Nowhere in any authentic scriptures, the definite high or low birth categorization has been done or mentioned any instance of the practice of untouchability.

It was the untouchability part in the ambit of caste-discrimination that was most degrading to human dignity. The worst form of discrimination where one is not allowed to drink

46 Wedding customs specified in the Vedas state that the bride and the groom should not have any common blood relation for 5- previous generations. This restriction ensured a very healthy offspring with better qualities as compared to the progeny of a couple that is closely related.

47 Gotra is the lineage. Every Hindu has a distinct Gotra, derived from their early ancestors. Marriage between people of same Gotra is prohibited to minimize congenial diseases and for better quality of progeny.

water from the common well or not allowed to visit certain place on account of one's birth.

No doubt, certain discrimination is present in every society. During apartheid era, whites had all the privileges and none for blacks or colored, the Jews and other non-Muslims are discriminated by many Middle-East and Asian countries; Muslims are discriminated in the western countries; Tutsis are discriminated by Hutus and vice versa. Shias face discrimination among Sunnis and Sunnis among Shias; Muslims and non-Muslims, American Blacks and Hispanics from Whites; Aboriginals in Australia, Armenians and Kurds among Turks; etc… the list is endless. And all these are birth-based discriminations. All responsible nations protect the disadvantaged citizens. USA has made laws to protect and help African-Americans. In India too they have enacted a lot of rules to enable the 'lower-castes' to help overcome the injustice of past years.

Today, all the discriminations all over the world have been legally disallowed (unfortunately religion-based discrimination is still followed in most of the Islamic nations against non-Muslims), but a newer discrimination has come in the play, the money-based discrimination. Today we worship money and hence moneyed people have higher status and therefore automatically a hierarchy has been established in the society and naturally the less-rich or poor get discriminated. In a high society club, everyone knows that they will cleverly avoid you on some ground or the other if your 'type' does not fit into their liking.

In the Vedic times too, the money had a status, but knowledge and discipline had higher status, hence even a penniless Brahmin enjoyed being revered by the rich and the powerful. It is not an accident that India today is the source of educated and skill talents of this world. The Vedic caste system was a system that ensured minimum discrimination. Mahatma

Gandhi, an avid fighter for the cause of the 'lower-castes' and the 'untouchables', subscribed to the Vedic caste system. However, it was the present-day caste-based injustice and the untouchability that prompted Mahatma Gandhi to distance himself from the currently perverted system saying: "I believe in the Varna-Ashram-Dharma in a sense, in my opinion strictly Vedic but not in its presently popular crude sense."

Untouchables

The concept of 'untouchables' was unknown in the Vedic times. The universal nature of Hindu Dharma that embraces every living beings; plants, animals, humans, an inclusive Dharma of this order can ever exclude anyone? However, we cannot ignore also a the fact that the untouchability did exist in certain quarters during later times.

All the 'lower-castes' were not 'untouchables' during even the worst period in the history. It was the 'lowest' among the lows, mainly the ones who were engaged in the profession as the butchers, the skinners, the cobblers, the undertakers, the toilet cleaners, etc. who came to be branded 'untouchables'. They were not allowed entry to certain places of worship, they were not allowed to draw water from the common village well, and their children could neither go to the school nor could mingle with children of other castes. They were considered so impure or so unholy that if they did come in physical contact, even by mistake, a 'high'-caste person will take head-to-toe shower! Untouchables were the last in the queue to receive anything; the least prioritized people. Indeed a worst form of apartheid system. Untouchability may perhaps have started for the reasons of hygiene, but it was a very inhuman and unjust system that needed to be demolished.

Reasons for Corruption in the Caste System

There must be many reasons, but mainly because Brahmins, proficient in Vedic-knowledge, who were the conscience keepers of the society, were prevented from guiding the society for many centuries during theocratic Buddhist interlude and thereafter foreign invasion that changed everything topsy-turvy.

The structure of the Vedic society began to alter with adoption of Buddhism as state religion by many rulers of the time. Vedic culture does not permit a theistic state, however under Buddhist kings, the theocracy showed its contempt to the upholders of Vedic traditions, the Brahmins. They were scorned at and were considered as unwanted poor beggars. The society even shunned them and stopped supporting them. Kumaril Bhatt[48], a highly intelligent Vedic expert and inspired by him the Adi Shankeracharya, after a Herculean effort brought the Vedic culture back in vogue, however the effects of hundreds of years of lack of effective educational and social service traditions of Brahmins had taken its toll. At that crucial time in the history of India, the marauding invaders from Central and Western Asia as well as from Europe came to India when the society was still in the process of repairing itself. It was again dealt a deadly blow, a couple of shades bigger.

Invaders of India from Alexander to the Islamic, Portuguese and the British observed that the strength of the Hindus was that penny-less, incorruptible, silent, Brahmin community. Being neither aggressive nor physically strong, Brahmins naturally were a soft target. They were identified and purposefully slaughtered.

---

48 Kumaril Bhatt was a scholar and an eloquent advocate of Vedic truths. He never lost in a debate with other philosophers. He wanted to open the eyes of the public to the truth, but could not succeed. In the end he invents a terrible way of self-sacrifice to wake up even the most insensitive. He decided to burn alive on slow fire of grain-husks to draw attention of all. At that time a passing young Sanyasi, none other than Adi Shankaracharya, sees the deadly spectre of Kumaril Bhatt seated atop a heap of husks which was already on fire. Shanker pleaded him to get off the heap. Kumaril Bhatt did not budge, but asked Shanker to complete his unfinished work of convincing people about living the life with Vedic codes.

Alexander, the first invader, came in BC 326, he, though failed to cross the river Indus, but isolated and killed all the Brahmins from the western border area of then India under his short-lived occupation. It was first genocide of Brahmins.

Incalculable damage was done by subsequent Central Asian invaders including Taimur, Changis Khan and Mohammad Ghori.

It is said of Aurangzeb, the Moghul ruler, that he had asked his chief of army to present to him every single day 20kg of 'holy-threads[49]' worn by Brahmins. This meant either the conversion of them to Islam or getting killed every day of about 4,000 Brahmins to recover from them, the 'holy-thread' that weighs about 5gm each. There were occasions when the collection was as high as 50kg. Muslim invaders and occupiers from Central and Western Asia too destroyed Brahmins. Most of the temples and Gurukuls that were seats of learning and dormitories of knowledgeable Brahmins were destroyed. This tale is so large, so cruel and so repetitively cruel, it numbs the readers. Suffice here to surmise that Brahmins had hardly any chance under the Muslim rule that lasted several centuries, to reflect upon the society and effect reversal of the caste-discrimination. These centuries were a period of hiding, lying low and of being content with plain survival of the Hindu culture. In rest of the world, wherever the ruler was Muslim, its population also became Muslim, either by force or by attraction of financial rewards by becoming the accessory to the king. India is the only exception in the whole world.

By the time Europeans arrived, hardly any Hindu educational institution was alive. The Brahmins could learn whatever they could only at home or under private

49 Holy-thread' is known in Sanskrit as Upaveet. In the Vedic period every man and woman used to be ceremoniously initiated into wearing it. Subsequently practice remained only among the Brahmins and Kshatriyas and as of now it is observed that only a few males among Brahmins and Kshatriyas continue to wear it.

tutorship of a few learned teachers. European occupiers also soon knew that the freedom-movement of India was mainly Brahmin-inspired and that the incorruptible Brahmin cannot be trusted and cannot be given position of authority in the administration. Brahmins thus treated, always under scrutiny, devoid of resources, could not fully maintain their tradition of learning and teaching. All this led to rapid erosion in learning and teaching Vedic education and Sanskrit.

The Portuguese occupation was especially more brutal and succeeded in significant elimination of Hindus from territories occupied by them. Even in their own country, Portugese were heavy handed on the adherents of other faiths. So fanatic Christians were they that a Portuguese himself, the great Philosopher Baruch Spinoza and his parents were not allowed back in Portugal until they renounced their Judaism and got converted to Christianity.

The British were not as ruthless as Muslims or Portuguese; they worked in a different way, perhaps in a more sinister way. They brought in an education system that ridiculed India and everything that India stood for. British government created an army of neo-educated Indians who looked like Indians but talked like British.

Unfortunately, the same education system with some cosmetic changes is still continued in Independent India. The vote-bank-politics has taken its toll and with an eye on votes of Muslims, Christians, Buddhists, 'lower'-castes, 'untouchables', communists, the centrist-socialist governments, have made the text-books and education system even more pitilessly against Hinduism, eliminating anyone from taking interest in the study of Hinduism and effectively stopping everyone from obtaining true understanding.

Muslim extremism (Talibanisation and Al Qaida inspired militancy) is at work in India and especially most aggressive in Kashmir that now stands almost fully cleansed of its

Brahmins (known as Kashmiri Pundits) in the regions of Pakistan occupied Kashmir, Chinese held Kashmir and the Kashmir Valley ('Kashmir Valley' is the part of Kashmir that is left with India). Kashmir was one of the most important regions for advanced learning of Hindu spirituality on account of traditions set by founder of Kashmir, a great ancient sage Kashyap and by the Kashmir's resident Goddess Saraswati, the Goddess of Knowledge. Most of the Hindu population of the Kashmir is known as 'Pundit' signifying 'learned Brahmin'. These people are killed, their women raped and the population made to flee. They are forced to migrate out of the state and live a life of refugees.

The Marxists and communist-inspired rebels and sympathizers are taking their toll on Brahmins elsewhere in the country.

Thus Vedic education suffered significantly. It is a miracle that despite efforts to destroy them, politically and physically, a small number has still managed to keep up their ancient tradition of learning and teaching, defying the onslaught.

Attempts to Rid the Caste-based Discrimination

What was the nature of the caste-based discrimination against 'lower' castes? Was it like in Europe where Jews and Gypsies were hunted by Christians? Where they were shunned from jobs? Where they were denied medical treatment by doctors?

No, the 'lower-castes' in India were subjected to a different form of discrimination. The 'higher castes' would give them the jobs, would never negatively interfere in their affairs and on many occasions even provide financial assistance to them. There was, and is even now, cordial relationship between both. The lower castes had 'respect' for the other and the higher castes 'needed' the other for doing their work.

The sense of discrimination started to appear when the 'higher castes' did not approve of the 'lower-caste' wanting to go to school, when he wanted to sit besides a higher-caste', when he wanted to go to the same well at the same time as a 'higher caste' and in general behave like a 'higher caste'. The marriage between members of these communities was unthinkable. We are familiar with the apartheid followed in South Africa, in erstwhile Rhodesia, where the white-people's residential areas, schools, railway train compartments, etc were out of bounds for the blacks and the coloured. Hindu caste-system, in its degenerated form, was almost like it, but short of written rules like those present in the apartheid countries.

Another difference was that the treatment received by 'lower-castes' was not uniformly applied at all the places by everyone at all the times. Brahmins kept a distance yet silently and sometimes openly helped them. Kshatriyas who had become land-owners treated them rather harshly (almost the way Whites treated the black slaves in Americas) and Vaishyas generally tolerated them well, however there were many exceptions too. This apart, in the areas where the system of land-lords was absent, the treatment to the 'lower-castes' was not physically oppressive.

Fortunately, the great spirit of ruthless search for truth and fair-play quintessence of Hinduism came to fore and literally hundreds of reformers started to work on correcting the anomaly. As a result, India has benefited from the reforms and huge strides have been made in empowering the 'lower castes'. Their members have climbed to very high positions in every field in the modern Indian society. Chief-ministerships, union-cabinet- ministerships and innumerable administrative positions in the government are held by them. One of the Presidents of India, K R. Narayan (1920-2005), was from the lower castes. Work, however, still remains to be done, not so much in terms of providing concessions and providing artificial props to them but by way of instituting self-inspired empowering.

Untouchables' plight could not be tolerated by many 'higher' caste intellectuals. They knew that the untouchables were not educated, were poor and could not help themselves. They have to be helped. Brahmins, Kshatriyas and Vaishyas, from the so-called 'higher-castes' have taken the lead to uplift the so-called 'lower-castes'. They have contributed a lion's share in this effort in raising a voice against this evil.

A Brahmin, Basveshwar (1134-1196), who was a great humanitarian, aroused a lot of goodwill for them. Another Brahmin, a Gujarati Saint-Poet Narasinh Mehta[50] (1414-1481), showered love and sympathy towards these discriminated 'lower caste' people by calling them as 'Harijan' (People of God) and even visiting their homes. A Vaishya, Mahatma Gandhi, who was champion of their cause, had named his magazine 'Harijan' after their name, coined by Saint Narasinh Mehta. Well known reformers, Swami Vivekanand and Swami Dayanand[51], had worked for uplifting of 'lower-castes'. As a matter of fact, every good hearted Hindu has denounced the caste-discrimination.

Belonging to the so-called 'lower-caste', Jyotirao Phule (1827-1890) of India's first Girl School fame, worked incessantly for the cause of the lower castes. Dr. Ambedkar (1891-1956), himself born as a 'lower'-caste who later converted to Buddhism, has created the constitutional provisions and laws in the Independent India to assist the lower-castes with out-of-turn allotment of university seats and government jobs so that the lower-castes can stand on their feet after centuries of suppression. Nearly all Hindu religious leaders have denounced caste-discrimination in public. Every political

---

50 Song immortalized by Mahatma Gandhi: 'Vaishnav-Jan to tene re Kahiye je pead parayi Jane re' (Call that man a Godly man who appreciates pains of others) was written by Poet Saint Narasinh Mehta.

51 Swami Dayananda Saraswati was born in a small town Tankara in the state of Gujarat. His original name was Mulshankar Dayal.

party has unequivocally denounced the caste-discrimination. Literally thousands of NGOs are ceaselessly working to eradicate the caste-based discrimination in India; the largest among them being the RSS, an organization of nationalists, they have declared their aim of ridding the Hindu society of caste-discrimination. They have publicly urged Hindu society to "take all necessary measures to ensure entry and access to every Hindu individual, irrespective of his caste, to their homes, temples, religious places, public wells, ponds, and other public places". All media, print, electronic or film, have tirelessly used every opportunity to curb it and to denounce it. From no platform whatsoever caste-descrimination is promoted.

When Will the Caste Discrimination Vanish?

'Lower castes' are a majority as compared to the 'higher castes', thus a substantial vote bank in a democracy. For garnering their votes, politicians of all colours are courting the so-called 'lower castes' with promises and more and more rules of out-of-turn admissions, promotions and quicker judicial fast tracks. It is now lucrative in India to remain a 'lower caste' and if you are not a born 'lower caste' than one would do all the tricks of the trade to somehow get 'legally' registered as a 'lower caste'. The 'Lower castes' stand politicized today and it has now become 'beneficiary' of the vote-bank-politics at the cost of the nation.

The ranks of 'lower castes' have started swelling. Referring to the swelling number of castes in the backward list, in a case, the Bench of Supreme Court headed by Justice K G Balakrishnan asked the government a searching question: "This means for 60 years (of reservation-policy), people who were disadvantaged continue to be backward. If this is so, then what is the meaning of the arrangements for social advancement of backward community for all these years?" It also asked the government: "Does the inclusion of a larger number of castes in the backward class list by the National Commission for Backward Classes (NCBC) indicate deterioration of their social status? Does a caste which gets designated as 'backward' and becomes eligible for quota benefits ever shed the tag? The Bench, also comprising Justices Arijit Pasayat, C K Thakker, R V Raveendran and Dalveer Bhandari, said, "Inclusion of a caste in the list would mean that it was previously socially advanced and did not figure among the backward class communities. But with time, their social status deteriorated and they had to be included in the list. This means more and more castes are getting backward as there are only inclusions and none being excluded from the list."

Mahatma Gandhi, who had real interest in the healthy development of the country, knew the result of an unmindful 'reservation-policy' suggested by Ambedkar, a leader of the 'lower-castes'. Mahatma Gandhi was against it, he suggested alternative by which the 'lower castes' could be provided financial assistance for better education so that one day, the 'lower' comes up to the level of 'higher'. When Ambedkar was adamant in his demand for reservations, Mahatma Gandhi agreed to it on a condition that the reservations would apply only for a limited period of few years. The Indian Constitution accordingly adopted a limited period one-time reservation policy for the lower castes. However, after Mahatma Gandhi's death, the short-sighted politicians kept amending the Constitution at periodic intervals to continue with the defective policy to keep their vote banks intact. It has become politically incorrect to speak against reservation.

Unfortunately the constitutional remedy has started to show up as what Mahatma Gandhi had feared that it was worse than the ailment. 'Lower' castes want to remain lower and if possible want to become even more 'lower'! It has become so murky now that even the 'higher' castes want to be lower because it is the reverse discrimination that has become an issue for 'upper' castes!

The politicians will not let public forget what their caste is, it is anyone's guess when the caste discrimination would melt away at this rate.

The Bhagavad Gita teaches that every caste is unique and equally important. As there are differences in every human, each caste has their own distinction and strengths. Every individual can take pride in his strengths and can utilize it for his own development. The caste-based discrimination and untouchability should be replaced by sense of pride based on the qualities freely available to every individual by virtue of his birth. As Hermann Heses observes, the differences exist even in Western world, whether one calls them by a caste-name or not. The practical way forward is to accept the differences, to capitalize them for self development with a sense of pride. This would automatically kill the demon of discrimination, without so much as even addressing it. Anyone can witness this change taking place silently but certainly in the work of Pandurang Shashtri Athavale. A feature film 'Antarnaad'[52], based on his work, has a tale-telling dialogue. A 'lower' caste fisherman who has realized his own intrinsic value as a human being, announces from a podium to a mammoth gathering, after regaining his self-esteem, that "All my life, I tried to act like a 'higher' class Brahmin, but now I say with pride that I am a fisherman. I want to be a first-class fisherman than ape to be a second class Brahmin."

Eliminate the caste-based discrimination but celebrate the differences, using the knowledge of Gita, thus removing sting of the caste-system yet retaining the system with its society-supporting features; the way it was meant to be.

---

52 'Antarnaad' is a Hindi film by Shyam Benegal. Antarnaad means 'the Inner voice'. In his testimony Shyam Benegal says that the film is based on true story of the transformation he saw taking place where the villagers are participating in the 'Swadhyay' movement inspired by Pandurang Shashtri Athavale.

Manu the Law-Giver, the Sage-King, a Great Kshatriya

English words 'human', 'man', 'woman' or German Mann etc are derivatives of the name of the king-sage Manu. The word Manu itself derived from Sanskrit 'Manus'. Hindu scriptures call Manu as 'the first king and the progenitor of mankind' (not in the sense of Adam, who was first created man by God), but in the sense that he was asked to repopulate and organize the world in aftermath of the Great Deluge.

Manu appears in every era. Era is also, therefore, known in Sanskrit language as 'Manavantar', the time period between two consecutive Manus. Current Manu is said to be 7th. Each Manavantar is several thousands of millennia (by some estimates, 308,448,000 years). Thus there are many Manus in Hinduism and they have played roles comparable to Adam and Noah in Biblical stories. Manu was a 'king-sage' who was forewarned of an apocalyptic deluge, is said to taken refuge at the present day Himalyan town of Manali[53] for safety from flood, kept intact all the previous knowledge (it is said that the knowledge of Vedas has been with us from earlier Manavantars) and rehabilitated the flood-ravaged earth. All those rehabilitated by father figure Manu considered themselves as Manu's subjects, his children. Therefore, we call ourselves the 'mankind' or in Sanskrit 'Manav' or 'Manushya'. He is said to be the law giver. His laws are known as 'Code of Manu' and they are collected in a volume known as 'Manu-Smriti'. Ancient Sanskrit grammarian Panini of 4th century BC defines a 'man' as that who lives by the laws of Manu.

Religious Conversions in Hinduism

In Hinduism, there is no formal tradition of 'baptism' or 'initiation' or 'Khitan' (circumcision) etc to be admitted as a

53 Manali was the name of Manu's wife, given to the town where they lived thousands of years ago. Today an Ashram still exists at the same place.

Hindu. If you are born in a Hindu family, you are automatically considered a Hindu.

Basically, Hinduism is a non-proselytising in nature. Hindus respect everyone's thinking ability and freedom of choice. Traditionally, they do not convert anyone into Hinduism unless he or she insists. Hindus, on the other hand, insist that everyone remains in his own religion and just evolves there to become a better human being.

Swami Vivekanand, at Chicago during the 'Parliament of Religions' in 1893, said to the assembly: "The Christian is not to become a Hindu or a Buddhist, nor is a Hindu or a Buddhist to become a Christian. But each must assimilate the spirit of the others and yet preserve his individuality and grow according to his own law of growth. If the Parliament of Religions has shown any thing to the world, it is this: It has proved to the world that holiness, purity and charity are not the exclusive possessions of any church in the world, and that every system has produced men and women of the most exalted character. In the face of this evidence, if anybody dreams of the exclusive survival of his own religion and the destruction of the others, I pity him from the bottom of my heart and point out to him that upon the banner of every religion will soon be written, in spite of resistance: 'Help and not Fight', 'Assimilation and not Destruction,' 'Harmony and Peace and not Dissension'."

If one is born in the other faith, or born in Hindu faith but converted into other faiths and wants to convert or return to Hinduism, priests do perform; although fundamentally, not essential, some basic 'cleansing' ceremonies to formally welcome those people into Hindu fold. Essentially, if you think you are a Hindu, you are. Nothing else is needed; no re-naming, no swearing-in, no pledge, no new rules, no new rituals, no special dressing, no fasting, no pilgrimage, nothing except your internal conviction. You become what you think. Indeed, the formal ceremony does help affirm your resolve. The formal ceremony involves, invoking a deity, witnessed by holy fire, where one announces his own resolve to follow Hinduism. He is handed over some holy books and appropriate scriptures in that small ceremony.

The process of religious conversion is a process of marketing; to show own product as superior, to hide its faults, to show other as inferior and to find (or even invent) faults in them. All the religious leaders, who are engaged in the activity of conversion, do nothing else but marketing, using marketing tools. Hindus, fortunately, cannot be faulted for condemning any religion as they do not get involved in the marketing of their religion. On the other hand, Christian and Islamic missionaries cannot escape this blame. Abundant material is available for one to see where Hindu Gods are denigrated by them, Hindu religious and social systems are ridiculed by them. Such material is widely created, distributed and propagated by the missionaries. It is not a coincidence that Mother Teressa in her entire career, spanning six decades in India, could not find anything good to talk about its ancient culture.

Islam and Christinity, both 'new products', originated in the harsh deserts of Arabian Peninsula. Their missionaries came to highly populated, culturally rich, materially wealthy India having abundant natural resources of every kind and began marketing their wares, denouncing Hinduism, the 'old-product'. Without the ability to comprehend what they were about to destroy, they zealously went about spreading their religion using every means, not waiting to consider even for once the loss mankind will face by denuding the world of the ancient wisdom distilled by centuries of research and labour. These both groups somehow thought it as their right to reform and recast Hindus in 'new' mold fashioned in the dry sands of cruel desert. They landed in India and began imposing their belief systems under patronage of their co-religious rulers who had rudely violated a civilized non-aggressive country. It did not occur to them that they are in the lands of others and that they should show some courtesy to the host. Why should they, when they have sword and gun in their hands? For them it was as clear as black and white. Hinduism is bad; it is their responsibility to save Hindus from the disaster of them being Hindus, who will never get salavation unless they convert and cease to be Hindus. As a visitor they came and both tried to become masters of this gentle people.

Mahatma Gandhi, who had during his travels within India and his interactions with millions of people, knew as to what the missionaries were upto. He had a great foresight. During the colonial days he gave a call to welcome those who had strayed away from the Hindu fold. He said: "If a person through fear, compulsion, starvation, or for material gain or consideration goes over to another faith, it is a misnomer to call it a conversion. Most cases of conversion have been to my mind false coin I would, therefore, unhesitatingly re-admit to the Hindu fold all such repentants without much ado. If a man comes back to the original branch he deserves to be welcomed in so far as he may deem to have erred, he has sufficiently purged himself of it when he repents his error and retraces his steps" (*'Collected Works'*: Vol. 66, pp. 163-164).

Mahatama Gandhi was outraged with conversions as he himself mentioned in the magazine *'Harijan'* dated November 5, 1937 that: "Only the other day a missionary descended on a famine area with money in his pocket, distributed it among the famine stricken, converted them to his fold, took charge of their temple, and demolished it. This is outrageous".

Mahatma Gandhi on Conversions

Mahatma Gandhi himself was under extreme pressure from his friends to be converted to Christianity. Rev. C F Andrews, a British and a minister at church, was his close friend. Mahatma Gandhi had several lengthy sessions with several Christian clergymen and active evangelizers. Some of the discussions are well preserved in the *'Harijan'* as well as the *'Young India'* and else where. He wrote on 13th March 1937 in the *'Harijan'* that: "My fear is that though Christian friends nowadays do not say or admit it that Hindu religion is untrue, they must harbor in their breast that Hinduism is an error and that Christianity, as they believe it, is the only true religion…so far as one can understand the present (Christian) effort, it is to uproot Hinduism from her very foundation and replace it by another faith."

On 3 June 1937 in *'Harijan'* he further wrote: "I am not interested in weaning you from Christianity and making you Hindu, and I do not relish your designs upon me, if you had any, to convert me to Christianity. I would also dispute your claim that Christianity is the only true religion".

He wrote in *'Young India'* dated 23 April 1931: "I disbelieve in the conversion of one person by another. My effort should never to be to undermine another's faith. This implies belief in the truth of all religions and, therefore, respect for them. It implies true humility."

In the 9th September 1935 issue of *'Harijan'*, he writes: 'I believe that there is no such thing as conversion from one faith to another in the accepted sense of the word. It is a highly personal matter for the individual and his God. I may not have any design upon my neighbour as to his faith which I must honour even as I honour my own. Having reverently studied the scriptures of the world I could no more think of asking a Christian or a Musalman, or a Parsi or a Jew to change his faith than I would think of changing my own."

In *'Harijan'* dated 30 January 1937, he wrote: "It is impossible for me to reconcile myself to the idea of conversion after the style that goes on in India and elsewhere today. It is an error which is perhaps the greatest impediment to the world's progress towards peace … Why should a Christian want to convert a Hindu to Christianity? Why should he not be satisfied if the Hindu is a good or godly man?"

Pope John Paul II on Conversions

Notwithstanding what Mahatma Gandhi thought about conversion, Pope John Paul II blatantly gave a call to proselytize in New Delhi in a public meeting attended by many dignitaries, including the then Prime Minister of India, a mild mannered poet Mr. Atal Bihari Vajpayee, on 7th November 1999: 'Just as the first millennium saw the cross firmly planted in the soil of Europe and the second in that of America and Africa, so may the third millennium witness a great harvest of this vast and vital continent'. Mr. Vajpayee, in the typically Hindu spirit, ignored the visitor's aggression. Going by the reports and webcasts of various Christian missions, the Hindus in India, Nepal and Sri Lanka are their favourite targets, having probably already met their targets in Mauritius, Fiji, Surinam and West Indies, where a sizable population of Hindus lived.

Hinduism, a Non-Institutionalized Religious Order

Hinduism does not subscribe to the idea of a central religious authority, such as what Vatican has in Christianity. They end up restricting freedom of speech, thought and action. Regulations are often passed by such a central authority to protect it and its office bearers, usually resulting in injustice, suppression of truth and infringement on personal freedoms. A great attention has to be paid by them on fund collection, asset management, banking, investment, insurance and general money management. The organization gets bogged down in pomp, propaganda, hierarchies, and lines of authority, salaries, benefits, lobbying and favoritism. Spirituality becomes a secondary objective in this process. Vatican has already experienced these pitfalls. And it continues to do so even now. Hindu philosophers and sages knew the perils of the institutionalization of religion, and their religion therefore has no central authority. Several thinkers, notably Mark Twain, have voiced their opposition to organizational religion.

Apparently disadvantaged Hinduism does not have any centralized body that could unequivocally opine, organize events or assist its followers. Another apparent disadvantage not so much to the philosophy but to its proclaimed followers is in terms of lack of any protection from onslaughts of followers of other faiths, who are sometimes insensitive and aggressive. To illustrate further, if Hindus are discriminated anywhere in the world, India included, who will voice their grievances? Who will take up their fight for justice? Who would extend support? Where can they go to redress their grievances?

There is nowhere to go for Hindus. But this is not a complaint. It cannot be. This is how it is and that is the price Hindus are ready to pay for maintaining their freedom of thinking, paving clear, unrestricted way to spirituality and inner strength.

With no help on anvil, Hinduism in substance should be strong enough to sustain itself on its own inherent strength of truth. The freedom to speak, think and act, gives the required strength to Hinduism. Thoughtful sages of the land of the Gita knew the truth that the Hinduism will survive the onslaughts. However hard it may become for Hindus, yet in the end an inclusive and open society where freedom of speech, thought and action is guarranteed and truth is held sacred, has to survive and prosper. The followers need to be brave and patient. Hinduism is the only religion in the world that claims no single founder, no single authority, and no date of its establishment and no exclusive book. It is nothing short of a miracle that despite adverse circumstances, in the midst of cruel aggressions and organized attempts to destroy it, Hinduism has survived for thousands of years. In spite of believing in no central authority or patrons, it has found ways to survive and has not lost its essence. In fact, it is said that this lack of patrons is a big reason why it could, for neither the rich, nor the powerful ever gain such a control over the religion so as to exploit it. For a Hindu his personal spiritual experience is more important than the dictates of a religious authority.

Perils of Institutionalization of Religion, Escaped by Hinduism

Different religious traditions meet the need of different people at different times, at different places and in different circumstances. However, when it becomes trapped into artificial or imagined boundaries, constraints and ambitions, it becomes a burdensome practice, devoid of spirituality. And in due course of time these religions lose their significance automatically; the artificial props cannot support a structure for a long time. The law of nature takes its course and resolves the issue ultimately. Even in our short historic perspective of a few thousands of years we have seen rising and tumbling cultures and their religions. Today's mighty looking religions also will have to prove the test of time. Whenever religious orders lose freedom of thought, reject the beliefs borne out of the enlightenment, lose the trust in the reason, the scientific world view, and the belief in the value of each and every human being, they become no more than mere sects protecting their vested interests.

At present, the institutionalized religions have fallen into this trap. Just as a police force has to hide its inefficiency, or a government has to hide its failures, institutionalized religions too have to hide their limitations and make it look like a still 'saleable package'.

Certainly, we know that Jesus did not start the tradition of Church and much less the concept of an institutionalized religious order. It was Paul who in his epistles made a major emphasis on the setting up of church traditions and including his own letters in the New Testament. Not only that Jesus said nothing about church traditions, he, in fact, condemned the Pharisees for that.

Institutionalized religions bring itself between the devotee and the God, becoming a barrier to his spiritual progression. It increases the fixation of beliefs to the detriment of individual experience. Automatically, the institutionalized religion will work towards codifying and standardizing the spiritual experiences. A devotee of God is degraded into becoming a devotee of man-made-Church, degradation from being a servant of God to the servant of Church, from a seeker of truth into administrator-manager of the institution, living and dying for it, on occasions cheating and lying for it.

Oppressive regulations, procedures and formalities, and orthodoxy somehow become part and parcel of such institutionalized religions. Spying on their own ministers, to ensure that they do not indulge in any immoral activity in the seclusion of the corridors of institutions, and if and when some ministers do indulge in unholy alliances, homosexuality or child abuse, the episode has to be contained, hidden and at worst to strike an out-of-court settlement by bribing millions of dollars. This all has to be done by the institution to save its 'image' and faith of millions of followers. From spirituality and God, they move to deceit and stealth.

When religion becomes institutionalized, its power vastly increases, both for doing good as well as for doing bad (even unintentionally, by having made a wrong judgment). History shows that these institutions have done more good to themselves rather than their followers. Because of their might they can endorse or reject ideas with massive force, to the detriment of truth or personal experience of the followers. For example, consider the long term effects of denying the place for women in the church. Or consider effects on the society by promotion of Islamic suicide bombers who are promised eternal paradise. Or consider religious intolerance of Rome that made extinct many ancient cultures and traditions of the world (Aztec, Viking, Celt, Mizo, Naga, Mayan, Red

Indian, Aboriginal etc.). When done by the mighty religious juggernauts, it is impossible for the non-conformist to survive.

Hinduism is neither institutionalized nor dogmatized. It does not have an institution that either endorses or rejects. For a Hindu, his own personal experience of spirituality is more important than what is said here, there or anywhere. Hindus do not have any centralized institution that can claim to have authority on everything Hindu. Most of their temples are stand-alone entities with their own individual priests or sanyasis (renuncient monks), unattached to any authority, be it religious or political. Even the mega-events such as the Kumbh-Festivals, where millions of devotees gather from all over the world, are not scheduled or organized by governments, temples or churches.

Threats to Hinduism from the Institutionalized Religions

Hindus in India have been feeling pressure on them for centuries from the missionaries of Islam and Christianity and of late they feel pressured from the state supported Indian communists and their sympathizers of various shades ranging from socialists to violent ultra Marxists[54]. Overseas Hindus are made to feel insecure in foreign theocratic states by denial of permission to practise their religion openly. There are many countries in the world that deny them building of temples for worship and facilities for cremation of the dead. During height of Islamic rules in certain countries, such as Afghanistan, Hindus had to identify themselves by wearing yellow coloured garments ensuring that they do not escape the treatment reserved for the 'idolaters'.

Many Hindus sense a danger of extinction and marginalization due to conversion of Hindus to Christianity or Islam by competitive religions. It has already happened

54 Ultra-Marxist, known as Naxalites, or Maoist, had publicly taken ownership of killing an old saint Lakshamanandji and running over his Ashram in Kandhamal district of Orissa in 2008.

in the North-Eastern[55] states of India, as the large population has converted to Christianity, the thousands-year old native culture, language and customs stand obliterated within a span of hundred years, demolishing the work done by their thoughtful and gentle ancestors and leaving unconverted small remaining population to face discrimination, deprivation, ridicule and insults.

Most other Hindus, who are not going so far as experiencing the danger of extinction, too are certainly aware of the marginalization and actually being ignored, victimized and ridiculed. Recent agitation in Kashmir, related to the Amarnath-Shrine is a good example of wanton disregard of Hindus in India. Amarnath is a place of pilgrimage in freezing Himalayas visited annually.

In countries where Hindus are a substantial minority and in India where they are still a majority, they are facing grim prospect of being ignored and deprived. The fear is real. With no 'God-fathers' to protect them, only God protects; and the God inspired individuals.

Non-Patronizing Hinduism

The way Hinduism is evolved it does not tolerate anyone patronizing it. Hinduism does not accept any 'boss' nor does it play as anyone's 'boss'. It does not recognize any one as sole authority nor does it authorize anyone to have sole claim on it. It is experienceable by everyone and everyone can contribute his knowledge and add to it, if not already there. This is the freedom Hinduism wants to enjoy. Not only because patrons spell peril in long run, they limit freedom of thought by inadvertent

55 There are seven states in the North-East region of India. According to the census report, from a negligible Christian following in the beginning of twentieth century, today Meghalaya has 75% Christians, Manipur 40%, Mizoram 90% and Nagaland 95% Christians. Effectively making extinct all local traditions, language, and way of worship.

subservience to the patron, however good or noble he may be. Freedom of thought being the super most characteristic, the history has hardly come across any government either today or yesterday or even in the distant past, who could dare to demean Hinduism by declaring it as an official state religion. Nepal was initially declared a Hindu Kingdom, but that was like an aberration, an exception. The new democratic government has deleted the word 'Hindu' from the name of the country. Thus, there exists no Hindu theocratic country in the world today. Hinduism and theocracy are antithesis. On the other hand, Islam is and was the state religion of almost all places where the ruler was Muslim or Muslims were in majority. As of date, there are 47 officially declared theocratic Islamic countries in the world. Same is somewhat true for countries with majority Christian population. Many are declared theocratic Christian countries. With the treaty of Secularism signed between Pope and the European rulers, now most of the declared Christian states follow secular policies, although their official state religion still remains Christianity.

Apart from freedom to think and act, another major advantage of the non-patronizing nature of the religion is its success in keeping the religion free from financial corruptions and unhealthy influences. Unlike what happened in Europe, where the rich could buy his space in heaven or buy a certificate of indulgence, in Hinduism, no amount of money can bend or change rules, shift a person from one caste to the other. No matter how rich one may be, he still has to wear the same holy thread made from cotton as everybody else, even though he can afford a gold-chain thread. The rich cannot influence stubbornly independent Hinduism, even if he was to donate millions in constructing a temple, he knows that he cannot request performing certain rituals reserved for someone else.

In the same way, the power of the powerful Hindu politicians or erstwhile kings too cannot influence Hinduism, even if he steps in to protect a Hindu. The religion does not ask him to protect a Hindu but asks him to protect an innocent, whatever is his religion. And his reward, if any, would accrue from God and not from religious leaders.

In Hinduism, there are no awards or rewards given by any religious or non-religious authority to the priests or to those who may have worked for the cause of Hinduism.

Quite to the contrary we have seen in the Middle-Eastern and European countries, kings subservient to religion and vice versa, cruelly and exploitatively manipulating the followers and punishing the opponents. It was common for the Church to sell 'indulgences' to amass billions to finance big monuments, churches and wars. And it was not uncommon for the kings to collaborate with Church to denounce their enemies as heretics and get them punished. There are literally thousands of cases where the kings have used the religion for their own selfish and often immoral or illegitimate purpose. And the Church has used king's power to fight its own battles. Church and kings collaborated during European incursions into Americas and Asia. During Islamic incursions, the spread of religion and political power always went hand in hand. The history is witness to those examples. This cannot happen in Hinduism. Neither the rich, nor the powerful can exploit the Hindu religion for their benefit.

Down-Side of Being a Non-Patronizing Religion

The down side of this great story of no-patron religion is the fact that it is not easy to find any 'Godfather' to save them. Unless a Hindu is downright correct and unless he can himself defend on his own merit, there is no other hope. Very unlike other religions and their followers who find ready help from official organs of their religions.

If Christianity is in peril or if a Christian is persecuted anywhere in the world, Vatican will extend help and so will other Christian states. Similarly, if Islam and Muslim suffer anywhere, Islamic countries would be very vocal and would come to defend. Israel would standby Judaism and Jews. Ironic, but Hindu will not expect any government helping on being a Hindu. No country in the world, including India will standby Hindus, historically, they haven't. However, on the individual levels, Hindus have received tremendous help, assistance and encouragement from individuals of all religions on account of innate fountain of human goodness, that God has distributed to the entire humanity in all corners of the world. Also, it is incredible, the number, if we were to consider how many great persons, who are not Hindus, but not only have, read the Bhagavad Gita, but have become its life-long ardent admirers, campaigners and followers.

Another down side of non-patronizing-Hinduism is that it does not have any significant commercial or political clout and consequently no media clout. How could that be? Where is money[56] to be earned in promoting Hinduism?

Among Vedic scholars, for the reasons of freedom of mind, it is considered to be below dignity to receive salary or gifts from the rulers. Some of the most illustrious Hindu sages have declined coveted state position even at the risk of inviting wrath of the rulers. A ruler well versed with Vedic traditions will not expect servitude from Vedic scholars; on the contrary, the ruler would be eager to follow his directives, as seen in Ramayana by king Dasharath who unfailingly accepted advice of sage Vashishtha.

Essentially Hindus are without political, financial, religious and media clout or cover. Despite this big vacuum, fearlessly they have roamed the world. Indeed, help always comes their way eventually. Their strength lies in freedom of thought, righteousness and excellence in their pursuits.

---

56 Tourism industry has discovered that religious tourism can generate good money for them due to sheer number of pilgrims and hence some form of investments are being made by corporates in recent times.

This is not to say that there is absolutely no help to Hindus. Individual Hindu charities were available from ancient times and are available even now. However, the main difference between Hindu charities and others lies in the fact that almost all Hindu charities are available to followers of every religion without any bias; Hinduism and biased attitude are antithesis. India has the distinction of housing world's largest number of charitable NGOs; most of these being unorganized mini charities. In past few decades, indeed some enthusiast have founded some charitable institutions, looking at the disadvantageous situation of Hindus, to help needy Hindus, however as yet they lack organizational ability; their naivety and failure to act coherently is visible. On occasions they are seen even working at cross purposes, hopefully it would improve with more experience.

Communism having failed as a viable social model is still not fully rejected by India. They are working overtime to bring disrespect to all the religions. While all other religions have some or the other 'godfather' in form of Church-group or Awqaf Board, Hindus having none are affected viciously by their unrelenting attacks.

On the other front, missionaries arriving from different countries of Europe and America started their schools along with Churches all over India. Although most of these institutions are listed legally as 'charitable' they do the religious activity. Young, poor and gullible are alienated from their roots and evangelized. This is unabated even under independent Indian administration as of now. As per the laws of Independent India, a charitable organization is not taxable but a religious organization is. Most of the church schools and related charities are legally registered as 'charitable' but perpetuate their 'religious' work unabated and without paying any tax that they should be paying legally.

Before Independence, British government of India had introduced an education system that had one objective, to produce clerks and officers to run the government machinery of that vast country. So that the natives should be loyal to the Crown, respect colonizer and hate their own countrymen, a clever system of education was instituted. This education system also negatively affects Hinduism.

Inspired by his evangelic father, Lord Macaulay (1800-1859) introduced in India in 1835 an education system where there was no place for Sanskrit language, Hindu scriptures, Hindu heritage and Hindu history. In addition to producing an army of clerks, it was devised to de-Hinduise the Hindus. Macaulay himself writes proudly to his father in a letter dated October 12, 1836: 'Our English schools are flourishing wonderfully.... The effect of this education on Hindus is prodigious. No Hindu who has received an English education ever remains sincerely attached to his religion. It is my firm belief that if our plans of education are followed up, there will not be a single idolater among the respected classes 30 years hence. And this will be effected without our efforts to proselytize; I heartily rejoice in the prospect.'

India became independent in 1947. Things changed a bit but more or less remained same as far as the cause of Hinduism was concerned. As a secular country, it is illegal for any religion to be taught in the government schools. While the Christians had their convents, Muslims had their Madrassas; Hindus had no credible or recognized Hindu school organization to bank upon. The British educated elites, who were happy to disown anything Hindu to become favoured employees of British, could not impart any Hindu education, even to their own children. Famous for his books 'Nineteen Eighty-four' and 'The Animal Farm', both satires on Stalinism, George Orwell (1903-1950) who was born at Motihari, in Bihar, state of India, had noted: "The most effective way to destroy a people is to deny and obliterate their own understanding of their history".

As a result, today most Hindu intellectuals, journalists, MBAs, businessmen, doctors, lawyers, engineers, teachers and the rest know hardly anything about Hindu philosophy, religion, heritage or history. Hardly have they known any verse from Gita, Vedas, Upanishads and Puranas. And to make the matter worse, they pick up isolated few quotes from the Hindu-bashers and flaunt their 'knowledge' adding to the confusion.

Even after all these, Hindus do not worry about a god-father, a patron! Indeed a brave faith.

Hinduism Survives Purely on its Own Merit

Having learnt the damage that has been already inflicted, many self-motivated individuals have now awakened and have started to promote the cause of Hinduism. And those more knowledgeable among the rest know that they have to pay the price for enjoying the freedom accorded by Hinduism to its followers. They do not complain: "Why no one comes to rescue Hindus in the way he sees the support forthcoming to any Christian or a Muslim". Hindus know that they have to help themselves and even help the whole world irrespective of what world does to them. Sounds unreasonable, but that is the way it is. And why not? God puts difficult questions and sets difficult tests for more mature pupils.

A Hindu to live, live well and to command respect, he needs to be sensitive, knowledgeable and efficient at work. In case, he is living in the midst of non-Hindus, he needs these qualities to be ever more pronounced.

In other words, a Hindu has to work around becoming a perfect human being, irrespective of what he is, what is his position, his education, his language or his colour. Others may be unjust, unreasonable, even down right cruel, but a Hindu must be balanced. Oblivious or not to this need, a Hindu mind powered by the strength of truth provided by the Hindu scriptures, never despairs. He is ever hopeful that the man opposite him would see the logic eventually; he does not need to take any short-cuts or detours from the root tenets of

Hinduism. Occasionally he does feel insecure, but that can be condoned. God helps who helps himself.

As long as mankind exists, their desire to explore and find the truth will exist. Thus a Hindu is self-assured; Hindus and Hinduism would exist till the human desire for truth exists. It does not need artificial life-support system borne out of institutionalization and patronizing by the rich and powerful.

Christians, Muslims and Atheists in a Hindu Majority India

World will recall the fact that when India was partitioned by British on the religious lines in 1947, Pakistan decided to go theocratic way becoming a Muslim country with Islam as state religion but in India, they decided to remain secular, recognizing all the religions equally. It was with more than about 90% majority of Hindus that India chose a secular constitution and with 76% Muslim majority, Pakistan chose to be an Islamic theocracy. It would perhaps puzzle people of the world, why a country officially divided on religious lines by British at the time of India's independence, chose not to be a theocratic state like its counterpart Pakistan and chose secular governance. This difference is due to inherently secular Hindu ethos. As Hindu theocracy is unthinkable, a contradiction in terms, unthinkable it is to see a secular Pakistan.

When Pakistan came into existence, it had two parts, consisting of current Pakistan and Bangladesh. At that time, West Pakistan had about 24% Hindus and East Pakistan (Bangladesh) had about 30% Hindus. Truncated India at that time had about 10% Muslims. In a span of 60 years of independent existence of the Islamic theocracy in Pakistan and Bangladesh, they have today just about 1% and 7% Hindus, respectively. What happened to the rest of their Hindus is easy to imagine. And look, in the secular India, Muslims increased their population from 10% to 14%. These tale-telling numbers! Also consider the fact that though both wings, East Pakistan and West Pakistan had one religion, they could not remain one. East Pakistan severed from West Pakistan through freedom struggle in 1971. On the other hand, although host to several religions, India still remains one country and still remains a secular democracy.

Attracted by its charm, several people came to India and still continue to come. They have written magnificent accounts of their trips. Also came hordes of invaders. Entrapped by its charm, many of these visitors settled down in India, never to go back. Today offsprings of thousands of Greeks, Huns, Shaks, Moghuls, Arabs and Europeans are inseparable part of Indian population. This together with existing populace following their own line of worship with range of variables gave rise to thousands of different traditions and thoughts within the overall Hindu practices. They all have lived together for centuries as inseparable entities, with a warm feeling of belonging.

Today's India has about 80% Hindus and yet they celebrate Christians, Muslims, Zoroastrians, etc as her Presidents, Prime Ministers, Chief Ministers, Chief Justices, Chief Election Commoners, Chief Attorney Generals, Chief of Army, Air Force and Navy! Nowhere in the world it is seen that population puts faith in followers of alien faiths in running their lives. They see as no offence if Buddhist auspicious symbol such as wheel (Dharma-Chakra[57]) on their national flag and the 4-headed Sarnath lion pillar on the official government documents.

Why is it that the parties advocating Hindu-interests and Hindu theocracy are not supported by the majority of Hindus? When India became independent, there were two religion based political parties; Hindu Mahasabha and Muslim League. Muslim League came in the existence for creating political power of Muslims. Even today they have some representation in the Indian Parliament with elected members. Hindu Mahasabha, too came in existence to create political power for

57 Dharma-Chakra is one of the 8 auspicious Buddhist symbols, others being, Conch, Lotus, Parsal, Water-pot, End-less Knot, pair of Fish and Triangle Flag.

Hindus, however, it stood rejected with no representative in the parliament. Hindus have shown that they do not like to support religiously-linked political parties, because of their inherent secular ethos.

Religious riots have indeed taken place in India, but in a fair view, aggression from Hindus has been rare phenomena, and been only after great provocations, and yet never justified or condoned by their leaders. Hindus are instinctively ashamed of the violence, even on an enemy. They would never utter the expression that 'they want to avenge' as some religious groups do.

Why are Hindus so generous to the extent of self-defeating, to perhaps a fault? This is so because 'Ishavasya Edam Sarvam[58]' (Everything is God-enveloped or God-wrapped) is core conviction of Hindus. It is not just casual, cosmetic, 'feel-good' 'policy' of Hinduism to respect other religious beliefs. Had it been just a superfluous cake-decoration, it would have been evaporated long ago in face of many trying situations that Hindus had to face during the historical invasions and colonization of India.

It is Hindu philosophy and its basic tenets that are deep rooted in Hindu psyche, which makes India, a Hindu majority country, to be religious and simultaneously committed secular and genuinely respectful to all faiths. And they will remain so forever, whichever political party gets elected in India. Even the so-called 'hardliner' Hindu political parties also cannot become un-Hindu by practising bias towards any particular religion. Hinduism forbids it. During the rule of Hindu king Shivaji, who was tormented by fanatic Muslim rulers surrounding his kingdom and who were killing Hindus and destroying temples, never practised biased policy towards Muslims living under his rule. Every subject of his kingdom enjoyed equality

American philosopher, historian and writer, Will Durant (1885-1981), in his book "The Story of Civilization: Our

58 This verse is taken from Ishavasya Upanishad.

Oriental Heritage", wrote in 1935: "The Mohammedan conquest of India is probably the bloodiest story in history. The Islamic historians and scholars have recorded with great glee and pride the slaughters of Hindus, forced conversions, abduction of Hindu women and children to slave markets and the destruction of temples carried out by the warriors of Islam during 800 AD to 1700 AD. Millions of Hindus were converted to Islam by sword during this period. There is no official estimate of the total death toll of Hindus at the hands of Muslims. Estimates have stated that over 13 centuries and over the entire subcontinent, the number of Hindus who died at the hands of the Muslims goes up into the millions. On several occasions, the Bahmani Sultans in central India (1347-1528) killed around 80,000-100,000 Hindus in a short period of time, which they set as a minimum goal, during their anti-Hindu campaigns. The massacres perpetuated by Muslims in India are unparalleled in history, bigger than the Holocaust of the Jews by the Nazis; or the massacre of the Armenians by the Turks; more extensive even than the slaughter of the South American native populations by the invading Spanish and Portuguese".

Historians have recorded chilling accounts of persecution of Hindus at the hands of Portuguese and British colonizers.

Despite all the sufferings, Hindus have by and large not hated their tormentors. India still maintains friendly relationship with the countries from where their tormentors came; forgetting and forgiving their misdeeds. Even with Pakistan and Bangladesh, despite their overt and covert animosity, India has always been first in building bridges. Religion-based massacres, persecution and hatred was mostly one-sided. Therefore, crusades and jihads were never needed by Hindus in their history of thousands of years; quite contrasting with bloody crusades in the short history of a less than two millennia of Semitic religions. Mark Tully, former-BBC correspondent, and proficient writer who has now settled in India, said very significantly that: "The genius of Hinduism and the very reason of its survival for so long was that it does not stand up and fight". Trusting inherent goodness in all people of the world, Hindus are world's perhaps the most forgiving people.

In the words of Will Durant: "Perhaps in return for conquest, arrogance and spoliation, India will teach us the tolerance and gentleness of the mature mind, the quiet content of the unacquisitive soul, the calm of the understanding spirit, and a unifying, a pacifying love for all living things."

Many centuries ago Jews entered India when they had to flee their homeland due to their persecution there. They were welcomed and they never faced any difficulty in India. Zoroastrian refugees landed in India after being cruelly dealt with in their homeland. They too were welcomed by Hindus. Muslims entered India as agressors and yet Hindus lived with them overlooking their atrocities. Christians entered India as aggressive evangelists to wean away natives from the 'false gods', yet they were respected. Everyone was provided every opportunity to prosper. In recent times, Tibetan refugees have joined the list of guests. Everyone is safe, Christians, Muslims, rest of all the minorities and atheists, in the Hindu majority India. They are not only safe but are thriving, one of the richest Indians being Azim Premji, a Muslim.

Toleration or Acceptance?

Hinduism is often described as a tolerant faith and Indian plurality is celebrated by everyone. But there exists a still grandeur quality of Hinduism to really celebrate—Acceptance.

Most world leaders today talk about it and urge their countrymen to be tolerant towards the followers of other religions. Is the 'tolerance' towards followers of other religions a great virtue? To 'tolerate' is to merely endure a situation or a person, one would ideally like to avoid. In that sense the word 'tolerate' smacks of negativity. In the absence of any other solution, the tolerance towards followers of other religion is made to look like a great virtue. But notice closely, they dare not talk about accepting other's religion as their own. For no religion other than Hinduism permits this. Vedic Hindu philosophy does not merely 'tolerate' but 'accepts'. It is no wonder that India is home to people of all religions (as well as of irreligious, atheists and anti-religious).

An inadvertent mistake is done even by the educated Hindus, who have not carefully understood the above difference. They parrot what they have learnt through their peers, who themselves were not well versed in the real Hindu thoughts of true universalism. They say that Hindus are very tolerant and they say that Hindus hold in equal esteem all the religions. Both these claims indeed true, but in their ignorance they are 'underselling' the greatest quality of their Vedic culture; where their forefathers had not merely 'tolerated' all but had designed the Sanatan Dharma to be able to accept all. It needs courage and power of truth behind taking this position, not found in any other religion.

Great Indian sage of our era, Swami Ramakrishna Paramhans, lived as a Hindu, as a Christian and as a Muslim turn by turn and realized the same truth. All the religions in essence want their followers to go towards divinity. The worshipping and praying to God is the divine part of all the religions. However, the decay starts when the religious leaders derive political, economic or social power out of their followers.

It is then that they want to defend their position of power and attack others, leading to competitions, leading to showing own religion to be better, leading to convert people by whatever means. They know that it is the devil that tempts and it is the devil that corrupts, but these religious expansionists do not mind using demon-technique and commit to treachery, violence and hatred to propagate their religion. Little they realize that in the process they are destroying their own good self into a degraded jealous, stealthy, greedy individual, far away from the lofty goals of their own religions.

Some missionaries deploy 'humanitrian' means of 'service' by providing food, shelter, medicines, education and employment. But a closer scrutiny will uncover their ultimate purpose. Mahatama Gandhi was very observant, he wrote in 'Young India' of April 23, 1931: "Conversion nowadays has become a matter of business, like any other...India is in no need of conversion of this kind... Conversion in the sense of self-purification, self-realization is the crying need of the times. That, however, is never what is meant by proselytisation. To those who would convert India, might it not be said, "Physician, heal yourself"". He further wrote in the same publication after six years, on 3rd April, 1937: "When the missionary of another religion goes to them (Hindus), he goes like a vendor of goods. He has no special spiritual merit that will distinguish him from those to whom he goes. He does, however, possess material goods which he promises to those who will come to his fold."

New Phenomenon, Assertive Hinduism

Inherently non-sectarian, embrace-all Hinduism is now thought by some of its adhersents to be under pressure and under threat of dilution, resulting into upsurge of defensive reaction recently seen as assertive Hinduism. With the advent of education and greater global awareness, Hindus have started to realize that powerful forces are and were at work against them.

The world still shudders in horror at the destruction of huge Bamyan monolith of Lord Buddha in Afghanistan at the hands of Talibans under full glare of publicity and attention and outcry of the world. Imagine then, what all atrocities could have been committed in the distant past when Islamic rulers had unrestricted access to any place and any home in India. During the rule of Muslim conquerors, millions of Hindus were killed, tortured and enslaved and their heritage was plundered, usurped or destroyed, just because they were Hindus. Hundreds of thousands of them were captured and sold as slaves in Central Asia and Middle-East. Gypsies of Europe are those Hindus who escaped from their Middle-East owners at great peril to their lives.

During their trips many of them died on the way (just as many negroes died when being mercilessly transported by whited hunters). The Afghanistani mountain range "Hindu-Kush", is so named because in Persian and Urdu it means "Hindu-Killer" (Kush is killer or to Kill as in Khud-Kush).

Among thousands of temples destroyed during Islamic totalitarianism in India, there were three most sacred ones; one at Ayodhya (the birth place of Lord Rama), second at Mathura (the birth place of Lord Krishna) and third at Kashi Varanasi (dedicated to Lord Shiv). These three sites are still partly or fully under Muslim control. Although there were hundreds of thousands of temples and Hindu holy places were captured, destroyed and converted into mosques by Islamic rulers of past, a non-political body RSS, representing a large number of Hindus and some other pressure groups made fervent appeals to Muslims to release at least these three places as a goodwill gesture towards Hindus. They also said that Hindus would forget and forgive all the historic crimes and misdeeds if they released these three sites for Hindus.

Muslim organizations ably supported by all the successive governments and armed with protection from secular Indian laws vehemently wowed never to give up those sites; gravely injuring sentiments of many Hindus. These factors worked towards the hardening of Hindu nationalism. Hindus felt that there had been no addressing or even acknowledging of their suffering and the injustice done upon them; neither by the authorities in power nor by Muslim and Christian groups. No gesture of recognition that Hindus had suffered came. That was probably the time; in 70s and 80s that assertive Hinduism took its roots in India.

Assertive Hindu Organizations

During British era, initially there was only one political party, the Indian National Congress, Indians of every shade and religion became its members to fight the British. Then on the political horizon, other parties too came up, drawing their ranks and files from the mother organization the Congress party. They were the Russian Revolution inspired Communist parties, British propped Muslim party (the Indian Muslim League to check-mate Congress) and Hindu party (the Hindu Mahasabha formed by dissidents from Congress party, who were unhappy with Muslim appeasement policy of Congress).

The Muslim appeasement steps were opposed by many Congress workers, who then resigned from the party and formed their own parties. Some formed political parties while some others went ahead to form non-political organizations to serve Hindus. The first non-political organized attempt was made in the year 1925 to unite Hindus by a physician turned social worker, Dr. Keshav Baliram Hedgevar. He founded a non-political organization called RSS. It is significant to note that although it was thought to have been meant for Hindus, he did not name it so and kept it open to all who considered India as their Holy Mother Goddess, keeping in mind the enshrined principles of Hinduism, founded on universal brotherhood of all humans. The name RSS (the Rashtriya Swayam-Sevak Sangh) means "the Group of National Volunteers".

Under the Umbrella of the RSS, many other organizations were formed to further the interest of Hindus and the nationalist Indians. Vishwa Hindu Parishad (VHP), Bajarang Dal, Akhil Bharatiya Vidyarthi Parishad (ABVP), Sewa, etc are non-political entities and the Bharatiya Janata Party (BJP) is a political party. Other smaller and regional political parties such as Hindu Mahasabha and Shiv Sena too play a role in projecting assertive Hinduism.

However, supportive of Hindus they may be, whatever protection Hindus may have had from these organizations, they are not universally accepted by all Hindus, once again proving fiercely independent and unpredictable Hindu mind. Hindus just do not tolerate anyone as their patrons.

What should be True Objective of Assertive Hindus

Hinduism does not tolerate patronizing. And Hindus do not like being huddled together as 'Hindus'. Have you seen a Hindu ghetto anywhere? They take pride in having their own mind. Hindu ethos has been that we are to look at every one with equal eye. How can a Hindu be partial to a particular community, or to any person? Even if it is his own? It is not in his blood to be protective about himself.

Muslims and Christians are known to have lived under orders of their religious leaders such as Pope, Khalifa, Mufti, etc since their inception, accepting their fatawas, proclamations and dictates. They can remain en-block, they can vote en-block, and they can fight en-block, but never would Hindus. Is it, therefore, any wonder that when two or three political parties suffice in any other country of the world that India needs 43?[59] Not one but four communist parties? This is hallmark truth, politically perhaps bad for Pro-Hindu politicians but makes perfect sense if one was to consider that the Hindu ladder of human progress is through total freedom of thought.

Hindus will unite, but only for much higher reasons, for loftier goals. They do not make themselves a commodity that can be traded by their union leader or political master. A church minister or a Muslim leader can help their followers make a choice, but that luxury is never possible for a Hindu Guru or Holy-man.

---

59 Officially, India has 730 political parties that are registered but not recognized by the election commissioner of India and 6 national and 37 regional parties (Total 43) that are registered and recognized.

'Secular' word was applied first in Europe when the interference of Church became excessive in the running of the governments. According to the treaty signed in Europe between Vatican and the prevalent governments of Europe, the Church was to stop interfering in the government affairs and the government would stop meddling in the affairs of the Church. Secularism does not mean disrespect and disregard to religion. This is true secularism.

Never ever in India, the temples meddled in the affairs of state. We in India were blessed since millennia by Dharma-sponsored secularism. Without needing the 'treaty of secularism', Indian was historically a secular polity. The artificial graft of 'secularism' in India was not even warranted. Its graft seems to have commenced a new meaning among Indian political elites. Secularism in India seems to mean becoming anti-Hindu; that is what at least it means to many Hindus. "Secularists" would do a great service to India in bringing together the split Indian polity by showing that they are not anti-Hindus.

Role of a Pro-Hindu leader is very hard in India. Because, Pro-Hindu also means pro-everyone! Even if everyone opposes him!

Mahatma Gandhi should be a role-model for Hindu leaders. He was a devout Hindu, read the Bhagavad Gita and led the prayer meetings everyday yet no one could brand him communal. He compelled Jawaharlal Nehru, a sworn enemy of RSS, Hindu Mahasabha and Bharatiya Jana Sangh[60], to invite 'pro-Hindu' parliamentarian Dr. Shyama Prasad Mukerjee[61], to the union cabinet; appointing him as a cabinet minister for industries and supplies. Mahatma Gandhi knew that the freedom was gained not only by the efforts of Congress party

60 Bharatiya Jana Sangh was a political party, a predecessor of today's Bharatiya Janata Party (BJP).

61 Dr. Shyama Prasad Mukerjee (1901-1953) was the founder of the Bharatiya Jan sangh.

alone but by every freedom fighter of every shade; he, therefore, wanted a 'National' government representing all major leaders and not an exclusive Congress party government, though it was INC who had clear majority in the first Parliament.

If only people of the world know what great idea the Hinduism is, no one will oppose it. I feel that it is this failure not to have shown the grand idea that Hinduism is, is the only impediment. We are drawn in meaningless competitiveness and petty-mindedness, forgetting the 'satyamev jayate'. With their correct conduct and correct presentation, Hindus could wow the world. People of the world are themselves a troubled lot, looking for solutions from their miseries, let us understand Hinduism in a better way and also help heal the whole world. Vedic philosophers have already given us the lofty target: "Krunvanto Vishvam Aryam", meaning, "let us make the whole world nobler". Vedic philosophers have even given us a lofty world-anthem (not just a national anthem): "Samani vah Akutihi, Samani Hridayani Vah, Saman Vastu Vo Manah, Yatha Vah Susahasati" meaning, "Let us all be one by heart and mind, let all our (literature, aims, arts) become truly beautiful and noble". "Sarvetra Sukhinah Santu Sarve Santu Niramaya, Sarve Bhadrani Pashyantu Ma Kaschit Dukhamapnuyat", meaning, "Let everyone become happy, Let every one become free from diseases, Let everyone be noble, Let there be no pain and let these even be visibly so". "Aum, Shantih, Shantih, Shantih" "O God, let there be physical peace, mental peace and spiritual peace".

Put the best foot forward.

Apology for Murder, Rape, Loot, and Destruction

Expressing 'sorry' and sensitizing the community that (at least in past) committed repression, gives the sense of justice (even if delayed) to the repressed. Wonderful precedents have been made by successors of Nazis and Imperial Japan to apologize for the war crimes. Church has in past apologized to the victims of abuse. They felt compelled to apologize on the strength of their own moral conviction. If today, Muslims and Christians in India were to rise above petty defensive psychology and were to share the agony of Hindus; surely their sensitivities would prevail upon them to do the right thing.

I believe that mere expression by Muslim and Christian organizations of recognizing maltreatment meted out to Hindus and the injustice done to them will instantaneously change the hearts and the minds of Hindus. I sincerely believe that if Muslim and Christian groups in India were to say 'sorry', it would make a sea change in the polarized Indian society. Honest little introspection will convince them to say 'sorry' to Hindus and that apology will go a long way in mending the relationship among all citizens of India. I can visualize that if anyone from these two aggressive faiths were to show courage to apologize, they would receive standing ovation from Hindu community. It will lead to an unprecedented reconciliation among all. As a recent example of improvement in the race relationship, look at the latest apology given by Australian Prime Minister Kevin Rudd in February 2008 to the native aborigines on behalf of white race for the indignity and degradation inflicted. The apology moved and brought tears in the eyes of indigenous aborigines.

Hindus do not comprehend aggressive Hinduism. Aggressive Hinduism is an antipathy to Hinduism, simply because Hindu religion is so open as to say that worship done to any of the Gods, ultimately reaches one God almighty. And that the whole world is one family. I believe the harmony between Hindus, Muslims and Christians is easy to obtain if some of their fair-minded leaders dare enough to simply express 'sorry' for the atrocities Hindus received in the past at the hands of their ancestors. I know this needs a very brave Muslim and abrave Christian to do it.

However, although artifical, this 'assertive Hindu phenomenon' has brought to fore certain issues out in the open. That is how India has witnessed some highly charged campaigns in last few decades on the issues of Ayodhya Ram temple and Cow-Slaughter. A term 'saffronization' is recently coined by the media to express Hindu influence. Saffron, in Hinduism is a color that signifies renouncing of material things, penance, sacrifice and service. Hindus celebrate all colors, Can the followers of other faiths recognize the crying need for becoming more sensitive to their fellow countrymen? Insensitivity is not a virtue. Jesus was Jesus because he was sensitive.

Hindu knows for a fact that he cannot and should not become so assertive as to become aggressive. Recent phenomena of Hinduism turning somewhat agressive will continue or will subside depends more on the action of others than on the Hindu actors. Hinduism is not an aggressive religion by nature. The staunch Hindu nationalist Nathuram[62] Godse (1910-1949), the assassin of Mahatma Gandhi, got no glory for his deed. A fundamentailst-Hindu or an extremist-Hindu is a contradiction in terms. It is very likely that aggressive Hinduism would cease to exist if the atrocities against Hindus are recognized and certain reparations towards them, made perhaps just a little 'sorry' would do.

62 Nathuram Godse assassinated Mahatma Gandhi on 30th Jan 1948 by firing three bullets from his pistol at close range in the chest of Mahatma at his Prayer meeting in New Delhi. Nathuram was member of Congress party till he was disillusioned by its Muslim appeasement policy. Later he joined Hindu Mahasabha. He did not defend himself during the trial. He confessed to the crime, was non-repentant and did not even take help from the attorney for his legal defence. In his submission to the court, he gave detailed account of why he saw no other alternative except elimination of Mahatma, he asked no mercy, and he did not allow any other person to ask for mercy for him and demanded appropriate punishment. He requested his ashes not to be scattered but kept securely to be emersed in the river Indus after Pakistan is reunited with India. He was convicted and was handed death sentence. He was hanged on 15-11-1949 in the Ambala Cantonment prison.

Cowardice or Stupidity of Hindus?

All civilizations all over the world have fought wars, subjugated territories, and enslaved people. Hindu culture stands out distinctly among all civilizations, being the one that have not done any aggression on their neighbours and on foreigners for thousands of years in an unbroken continuity. Was that the cowardice or the stupidity of Hindus? Or is it that we are making out a virtue of the cowardice?

Karl Marx thought it as strange, and perhaps just short of stupidity. Writing in the New-York Daily Tribune, August 8, 1853 he summed up: "Such a country and such a society were they not the predestined prey of conquest? If we knew nothing of the past history of Hindostan, would there not be the one great and incontestable fact that even at this moment India is held in English thralldom by an Indian army maintained at the cost of India? India, then, could not escape the fate of being conquered, and the whole of her past history, if it be anything, is the history of the successive conquests she has undergone. Indian society has no history at all, at least no known history. What we call its history, is but the history of the successive intruders who founded their empires on the passive basis of that unresisting and unchanging society. The question, therefore, is not whether the English had a right to conquer India, but whether we are to prefer India conquered by the Turk, by the Persian, by the Russian, to India conquered by the Briton".

Puzzled foreign historians still wonder as to how the non-aggressive Hindus had for thousands of years a very strong influence on cultures and languages of Indonesia, Malaysia, Thailand, other South East Asian countries, without any historical record of active push, wars, or religious evangelic efforts by them. A British historian, unable to fathom the reason for such a close link between the cultures, wrote in his book on the history of South-East Asia, that among Hindus, as there was no spirit of adventure or bravery enabling them to go out and enforce their culture, it was the natives of these (SE Asian) countries who themselves went to India and learnt their culture and having found it impressive, adopted it!!

Another historian wrote about a Rajput king of Delhi, Prithavi Raj Chauhan (1168-1192), and described him as a naïve and stupid. Prithavi Raj got this label because he pardoned Muslim invader Mohammad Ghori (1162-1206) repeatedly in the hope that he would mend his ways eventually. As per some historians, Ghori attacked India a number of times and his army was repeatedly beaten back. Mohammad Ghori was repeatedly taken as a prisoner. Highly cultured and kind hearted Prithavi Raj Chauhan had set him free every time he was imprisoned after he vowed not to attack again. Ghori did never keep his word; he made one more attempt, familiar now with all the defence strategies of Prithavi Raj, and succeeded in defeating him. Ghori is credited as founder of the first Muslim empire in India.

The roots of generosity and sense of fair-play is derived by Hindus from the time immemorial. They are inspired by lofty pattern of behaviour demonstrated by their ancestors. Hindus only care for the duty, whatever be the consequences.

In the ancient times, after defeating Lankan King Ravan, the victor Lord Rama, gave away the kingdom to Ravan's brother, Vibhishan. Same Lord Rama who was crown prince of Ayodhya, gives up the throne on the very day of his coronation and walks away to years of wandering in forests.

Brother of Lord Rama, the King Bharat, ruled in absence of Lord Rama, but had vowed never to sit on the throne. He never sat on the throne of Ayodhya, but kept it secured for his brother Lord Rama to return from his wanderings of 14 years. King Bharat relinquished his role as a care-taker-king as soon as Lord Rama returned.

Inspired by the guidance received from Lord Krishna, Pandavas, having won the Mahabharat battle, ruled for

36 years the length and breadth of India (boundaries stretching from present Iran-Afghanistan in west to Myanmar in east; from Kashmir in north to Shri Lanka in south). In the end, they handed over the empire to their succesor, Parikshit and decided to spend the rest of the time as hermits in Himalayas, giving up every worldly pleasure and to die there all alone in the contemplation of God.

In another incident, much before Mahabharat, Lord Vaman drove away King Mahabali from his kingdom in South India but instead of himself becoming the king, gave the kingdom to Mahabali's son Danasur.

The latest was giving up of Bangladesh by India after winning that territory from Pakistan in December 1971.

Hindu history is unique with no parallel in the world. Where else can one find thousands of renunciant kings and victors who had willingly forsaken their power and wealth?

Hinduism teaches to share, not accumulate. Give, not take and the whole mankind is one family. This education detoxes them of vengeanceful attitude and teaches them voluntary limits on their greed. We misunderstand someone's modesty as his stupidity, someone's tolerance as cowardice, someone's charity as foolishness. Proverb says that among the naked the clothed looks stupid. People measure with their own yardsticks.

Jesus said in the Sermon on the Mount: "You have heard that it was said, 'An-eye-for-an-eye, and a-tooth-for-a-tooth.' But I tell you, do not resist an evil person. If someone strikes you on the right cheek, turn to him the other also. And if someone wants to sue you and take your tunic, let him have your cloak as well. If someone forces you to go one mile, go with him two miles. Give to the one who asks you, and do not turn away from the one who wants to borrow from you". Undoubtedly, we would call that man stupid if he actually follows what Jesus Christ preached on the Mount. In a world where believers of 'eye-for-an-eye and tooth-for-a-tooth' are many, follower of

Jesus may look stupid or cowardly. Conviction borne out of great compassion, brotherhood and bravery are needed for such behaviour.

Hinduism's opennes, its forgiving attitude, its non-patronizing, its non-institutionalizing, its freedom of thought, its freedom to choose way of worship, its freedom to choose deity, its attitude of renunciation and its sense of performing duty without asking for rights is borne out of a highly developed and matured Vedic culture having a unique thought process. Because no where in the world, its equal is found, it may look strange.

Is it cowardice? Is it stupidity? Or is it a language of an evolved culture to shame the perpetuators of brute force? All said and done, look, despite all the hits Vedic culture received, it is the only among the ancient civilization that is still standing tall, still alive, still pulsating with vitality, still a source of inspiration to the whole world and still based on same ancient principles, undiluted.

Open Society Founded on Vedic Principles

In the older among all Vedas, the Rig-Veda, we find one of the most profound declarations of timeless advice that has moulded Hindu minds. "Let the noble thoughts come to me from all directions". Mahatma Gandhi said in 'Young India' dated 1 June 1921: "I do not want my house to be walled in on all sides and my windows to be stuffed. I want the cultures of all lands to be blown about my house as freely as possible. But I refuse to be blown off my feet by any. I refuse to live in other people's houses as an interloper, a beggar or a slave."

In Sanskrit, the very meaning of the word "Veda" is "Thought" or "Knowledge". A linguist will see the easy connection between the Sanskrit 'Veda' with similar meaning of Greek word 'Voida' (meaning 'I know') or Swedish 'Veta' (meaning 'to know'), Latin 'video' (meaning 'I see'), Czech 'vidim' (meaning 'I see').

For Hindus, the freedom of thought is 'the' most important. It is so ordained by the scriptures and automatically inculcated in their personality by autosuggestions, metaphors and traditions. A devout Hindu while performing his daily prayers or worship puts vermillion on his or her forehead as a mark of respect for the "power of thinking" that is resident in the brain and as his commitment never to surrender his intellect. At 10-35, the Gita states that "the divine among verses is the Gayatri Verse". That verse of much older antiquity than Gita, states: "God, illumine our mind and inspire us to divinity". Holy thread worn on the torso by Hindus reminds him of his commitment to respect and uphold the Vedas, knowledge and the knowledgeables.

The Vedas are considered by historians as the most ancient of the texts found anywhere. Hindus believe that the knowledge of Vedas has been in existence for thousands of years, even before the great cataclysm. Historians have come up with widely differing dates because a precious little historical or archaeological information has yet been uncovered. Although some have dated it to 6500 BC, other experts concede it to be of much more antiquity. Vedas have always had an oral communication tradition; going far beyond the earliest written evidence that historians have found. The written material tends to get destroyed over a period of time. On the other hand, the material in spoken poetry form, passed from one generation to the next, outlasts attempts of destruction and decay. Another intrinsic character of Sanskrit language has helped the ancient verses remain uncorrupted forever. In Sanskrit, the poet has to follow certain rules in construction of poetry. Not only the language of the poetry should convey meaning intended by the poet, but even its text structure is more or less fixed in terms of number of letters, words, vowels ('Matra' in Sanskrit), Raga etc, thereby virtually making it impossible to corrupt even in a long-long period. This is the secret of guaranteed fidelity of the ancient Hindu scriptures.

3

Place of Bhagavad Gita in Hindu Scripture: Ancient Hindu Scripture

Ancient Hindu scripture is divided into two main categories, the 'Shruti' and the 'Smruti'.

Shruti

Shruti is 'that which is heard (from divine sources)', it is considered 'timeless' and divine. In the hierarchy of admissible evidences, Shruti has the foremost place.

All the Vedas and the Upanishads are classified as 'Shruti', because their construct is considered super-human in the sense of 'flaw-free'. They are also known in Sanskrit as 'Apaurisheya' meaning 'impersonal' or 'beyond human ability'.

There are only four Vedas: Rig-Veda, Sama-Veda, Atharva-Veda and Yajur-Veda.

'Upanishads' are discussions and dialogues further elucidating Vedic knowledge, nature of God, Soul ('Atma'), Supreme Soul ('Paramatma'), Body, Mind, Liberation ('Moksha', 'Mukti'), etc. There are about 200 Upanishads, all classified as 'Shruti'. Of these 11 are considered as principal Upanishads and are more commonly read. These are: Aitareya-Upanishad, Brahadaranyaka-Upanishad, Isavasya-Upanishad, Taitteriya-Upanishad, Kath-Upanishad, Chandogya-Upanishad, Ken-Upanishad, Mundak-Upanishad, Mandakya-Upanishad, Prashna-Upanishad and Svetasvatara-Upanishad.

'Upanishad' in Sanskrit means 'the knowledge obtained sitting at the feet of the Master'. They are also known as 'Vedant', the 'Culmination of the Vedas'.

It is to these Upanishads that Arthur Schopenhauer, the German philosopher, referred to as "the solace of his life and the solace of his death". When talking about his famous work "The World as Will and Representation" he says that: "If then the reader, I say, has received his initiation in primeval Indian wisdom, and received it with an open heart, he will be prepared in the very best way for hearing what I have to tell him. It will not sound to him strange, as to many others, much less disagreeable; for I might, if it did not sound conceited, contend that every one of the detached statements which constitute the Upanishads, may be deduced as a necessary result from the fundamental thoughts which I have to enunciate".

The Bhagavad Gita qualifies as 'Shruti' owing to its divine origin and its dialogue-form, and easy style.

Although in existence, in study and in practice, for thousands of years in the East, the West's exposure to the Vedas and Upanishads and to its organized study started only recently. Thanks go to the translations of Hindu texts done by the Moghal Prince Dara Sikoh[63] (1615-1659), and the French writer Anquetil du Perron for this.

Dara Sikoh wanted to reconcile Hindu spiritual thoughts with the Koran and in that pursuit, he learnt Sanskrit to translate the Upanishads into Persian. Book of that translation was known as "Sirre-Akbar" (The greatest Mystery). 'Sirre-Akbar' was translated into Latin by French writer Anquetil du Perron and was thus exposed to European readers for the first time during Eighteenth century. Perron was so impressed by Upanishadic philosophy that he called them 'the production of the highest human wisdom' and considered them to contain almost 'superhuman conceptions'.

63 Dara-Sikoh, was the eldest son of Emperor Shah Jahan. He was killed by his younger Aurangzeb.

Smriti

Smriti is 'that which is recollected or remembered'.

'Purana', 'Laws of Manu', the "Manu-Smriti" and 'Itihaas' are classified as 'Smriti.'

There are eighteen main Puranas and an equal number of subsidiary Puranas or Upa-Puranas.

The main Puranas are: Vishnu-Purana, Naradiya-Purana, Bhagavat-Purana, Garud (Suparna)-Purana, Padma-Purana, Varah-Purana, Brahm-Purana, Brahmanda-Purana, Brahm-Vaivarta-Purana, Markandeya-Purana, Bhavishya-Purana, Vaman-Purana, Matsya-Purana, Kurma-Purana, Ling-Purana, Shiv-Purana, Skand-Purana and Agni-Purana.

The Itihaas is 'that which was', in other words, the 'history'.

Mahabharata, Ramayana etc are classified as Itihaas. Keen reader will note that, the Bhagavad Gita, is though a part of the Mahabharata, an Itihaas, is having status of Upanishad (which is a 'Shruti') in the ancient Indian literature.

The Author and the Scribe of the Bhagavad Gita

History narrated in Mahabharata is authored by vada Vyas. But it has been penned down by Lord Ganesh[64]. It is believed that Vyas was looking for a rapid writer, a scribe, who could take up the challenge of writing fast at the speed of his dictation. Lord Ganesh, known for his prowess at writing, takes up the challenge. Vyas spoke and Lord Ganesh wrote the entire Mahabharata, inclusive of the Bhagavad Gita. It is believed that they wrote down and created the massive work of 100,000 verses sitting in a place near the present-day village known as Mana Gaon, near Badrinath town in the midst of Himalayas.

Father of VedaVyas was a great sage, Parasher, and mother Satyavati, a fisherwoman. Vyas was born on an island in the river

---

64 Lord Ganesh is believed as patron deity of Wisdom and balanced outlook

Yamuna. Because he was born on an island, he is also known by another name, Dvaipayan[65]. Vyas had dark skin; hence he is also referred to as Krishna[66]-Dvaipayan. Reverentially, it is said of great sage Vyas, saluting his prolific writings, that: "Vyas Uchhista Jagat Sarvam". This expression is un-translatable in any western language as there exists no equivalent of the word 'Uchhista', however, the expression poetically conveys the meaning that "there exists no subject that Vyas has not tackled."

The Bhagavad Gita Embedded in the Mahabharata

Most of the 700 verses of Bhagavad Gita are spoken on the battlefield of Kurukshetra, a location in the present-day Haryana State of India, about 160 km north of New Delhi. In an area that covered about 148 km in circumference, two rival armies are standing; eyeball-to-eyeball distance in front of each other, ready to march and kill the opponents at the sound of the war-bugle. Both are mighty armies with renowned line-up of great warriors, Kaurav side had 2.4 million soldiers (11-'Akshauni'[67] army) and the rival Pandav, had a lower count of 1.5 million warriors (7-'Akshauni' Army). Both armies are described in the great epic Mahabharata as the 'Chaturangi', meaning having all the four elements; Elephants, Horses, Chariots and Foot-soldiers.

Known as the Mahabharata War, that is just about to erupt, would be consuming 3.9 million lives in 18 days.

Battle-ready Pandav prince Arjun asks his charioteer to drive his chariot and place it in between the two standing armies, so that he can inspect both the armies. This Great War is described

65 Dvaipayan: In Sanskrit, 'Dvip' denotes 'Island'. Dvaipayan is 'came from island'.

66 Krishna: in Sanskrit the word Krishna means 'dark' or 'black'. Lord Krishna also was so called, because of his dark skin colour.

67 Akshauhini' is an ancient term similar to 'Army-Division', indicative of a major unit of an army. Each Akshauhini has 21,870 chariots with chariot-riders, 21,870 Elephants with riders, 65,610 horses with riders and 109,350 foot-soldiers (in a ratio of 1:1:3:5), that is about 220,000 soldiers in one Akshauhini .

as bloodiest in the history of mankind, bloodier[68] than both the world wars put together.

The Kaurav monarch Dhritrashtra who is blind and who is tense about the fate of his children, the Kauravs, in the war, is in his palace, listening to the running commentary of the war by Sanjay, his charioteer and assistant. Sanjay has some means of being able to see and hear what is happening on the war front, akin to present-day communication system. Mahabharata epic calls that equipment simply as 'Divine eye', loaned to him by sage Vyas, a power of clairvoyance. And this is the beginning of the Bhagavad Gita. The first verse starts with a question from Dhritarashtra, asking Sanjay to tell him as to what is happening at the war front. Sanjay starts to give him the position of various formidable warriors, known for their frightening prowess in war.

Krishna is a cousin to the Pandavas. He was a leader of the 'Vrushni Sangh' (Federation of States of Vrushni Yadavas). Until this point in Mahabharata, Krishna is known as a knowledgeable and important person. It is only later that he becomes known as 'Lord Krishna'. He had a special liking for Arjun and admired his humble, principled, enthusiastic, energetic and intelligent nature. He participates in the battle from the side of the Pandavas. However, Lord Krishna had made a condition[69] that he would not use weapon in the war. Arjun requests him to drive his chariot in the war.

---

68 Casualties of 3.9 million in Mahabharat War took place only in 18 days (that is 1,800 soldiers every minute, as compared to 570 per minute in the First World War and 900 per minute in the Second World War).

69 Both, the Kauravs and Pandavs had approached Lord Krishna for help in their war against each other. Krishna had made a condition at that time: either entire army of Vrushni Sangh or just the weapon-less, non combatant Krishna himself. He asked them to choose. Arjun being younger than Duryodhan, it was proposed that first right of choice should be given to the younger. Arjun single mindedly chose weapon-less Krishna. This gave much delight to Duryodhan who wanted the mighty army of Vrushni Sangh, and got it.

Isn't it truly perplexing that the holy book is set in this grim and bloody setting? It is even more perplexing when we hear the hero of the peaceful Satyagraha movement; the apostle of peace, the legendary Mahatma Gandhi took his inspiration from the verses spoken in the middle of 'mother of all battles'? He said: "When the disappointment stares me in the face and all alone I see no ray of light, I go back to the Bhagavad Gita. I find a verse here and a verse there and I immediately begin to smile in the midst of overwhelming tragedies" This perplexity in itself is a solid and compelling reason for one to examine its content.

Mahabharata has 100,000 verses. There is a chapter called 'Bhishma-Parva'. The Bhagavad Gita is a tiny part of Bhishma-Parva.

In the classification of ancient literature, the Mahabharata is classified as 'Itihaas' (history) and not the 'Shruti', however due to its huge size and inclusion of a vast range of knowledge presented within it some describe it reverently as the 'fifth Veda', a 'shruti', though technically it is not.

A terrible war is fought between the cousins, the hundred Kauravas and the five Pandavs. But the Mahabharata is not just about the war but even all the events of yore leading up to it. 'Maha' means 'Big' or 'Great' or 'Greater' and 'Bharat' means 'a country that is named after King Bharat, (that is India). Joined together, the Mahabharata simply means 'Greater India', but in its book form, the word 'Mahabharata' implies, 'The book of the history of Greater India'.

Why the war was fought and who were the Kauravas and Pandavas etc details are supplied in the voluminous "Mahabharata". But here is the briefest possible version:

India was ruled by Pandu (the father of the Pandavas) belonging to the 'Kuru' dynasty. Upon his premature death, his brother Dhritarashtra (Father of the Kauravas) was asked to become the replacement king. But as Dhritarashtra was blind, his hundred children wielded all the power by proxy. Dhritarashtra knew of illegitimate usurpation of power by his sons but kept mum lest his children become unhappy with him. This was very unfair to the legitimate heirs of the throne, the 5 children of Pandu, collectively known as 'Pandavas'. But under the circumstances, being children of current king, the Kauravas also are technically eligible heirs to the throne. The vexed problem of inheritance was amicably solved by wise and experienced Bhishma who was the senior-most member of the Kuru dynasty, and its sworn protector, a most respected elder. Bhishma, to be fair to everyone, and to have peace among the cousins, split the kingdom equitably among the Kauravas and the Pandavas.

According to the arrangement, half of the kingdom was to be ruled by Kauravas and the other half by Pandavas. As the history goes; through a lots of twists and turns, in a game of dice, the stake is the kingdom and compulsory stay of 13-years[70] in exile away from kingdom. Pandavas lose the game, thanks to expert dice manipulator uncle of Kauravas. As per the conditions of game, the Pandav brothers leave the palace for the forest. When they return to Hastinapur (the capital of Kaurav kingdom) after 13 years of exile, fulfilling every condition, the Kauravas treacherously refuse to return their kingdom. Being virtuous, although shocked by the betrayal, Pandavas were not interested in fighting with their own kiths and kins. They spent a lot of time peacefully persuading the Kauravas. Under the guidance from legendary Lord Krishna, they showed remarkable patience and accommodation. They even showed the willingness to settle for a fraction of their legitimate territory, just five small villages, anywhere, even in the far off

70 Out of 13 years, 12 years have to be spent in forest and thereafter 1 year in hiding. If they are discovered during the period of hiding then they had to repeat 13 years of exile Idea was to get rid of Pandavas, by cheating in the game of dice using an expert dice manipulator and deceiver Shakuni, an uncle of Kauravas, the king of Gandhar (Present-day Kandahar in Afghanistan).

wasteland. But in their arrogance, Kauravas, controlling the length and breadth of India, did not agree even to this request of a tiny territory. On the other hand, they rubbed the salt to the injury stating that they will not give a piece of land even as tiny as the point of a needle; and if Pandavs have any guts, let them fight, and win their part of kingdom in a war instead of behaving like beggars. Pandavas were challenged and had no other alternative except war. However, Lord Krishna prevailed upon them to let there be one more peace attempt before coming to any drastic conclusion. In a final attempt at reconciliation, Lord Krishna Himself tried to broker peace, but power intoxicated Kauravas did not relent.

Pandavas were wronged, they were cheated, were insulted and challenged into war by 'Adharmi', the unrighteous one. The issue was now to be settled only by the war for justice to be delivered.

With the help of allies, the Pandavas drafts in an army consisting of seven akshauhinis and the Kauravas put together an army of eleven akshauhinis.

This is the background to the Mahabharata War.

And now minutes tick before the battle is to begin, Arjun, who had meticulously planned for this war now suddenly feels confused, he does not want to fight his own relatives and says that he would rather prefer to be killed weaponless, unresisting, instead of killing relatives. He tells Lord Krishna: "My senses are overcome by the weakness of pity, and my mind is confused about duty (Dharma). Please tell me what is righteous for me. I am your disciple, and I take refuge in you." Krishna addresses Arjun's dilemma to enable him to decide what path he should take.

The Date of the Bhagavad Gita

Historians have been giving differing opinions on when the Bhagavad Gita came into existence. The time periods suggested range from 4000 BC to 0 BC. According to the studies made by legendary mathematician and astronomer Aryabhatta[71] who lived in the 5th century, the Mahabharata War and hence Gita, can be dated to the 3-4 millennium BC. It is thus accepted by most as about 5000 year-old piece of poetry.

Hindus and indeed the wider audience have realized the timelessness of Vedic wisdom. Swami Vivekanand very aptly says that dates are unimportant for the study of the Gita. Unavailability of dates is a usual complaint about not only the Gita, but about almost every ancient Hindu literature. We can only speculate that either because Hindus gave more importance to the substance of the wisdom than the dates or that the wisdom is truly of so much antiquity that dates are lost centuries ago.

Nothing Worth Knowing Remains to be Known

The sentence "Nothing worth knowing remains to be known" smacks of arrogance. However, when one has understood the Bhagavad Gita; the reader will then know why Albert Einstein said, "When I read the Gita, and reflect about how God created this universe, everything else seems so superfluous". That was not in arrogance; that is not the same as what Caliph Omer said, who ordered the destruction of the Library of the Alexandria and the burning of all its books in the year 642 A.D. In his own words, "They (the books) will either contradict the Koran, in which case they are heresy, or they will agree with it, so they are superfluous". The books and scrolls were taken out of the library and distributed as fuel to the bathhouses of the city. So enormous was the volume of literature, they say, that it served six months, heating the saunas of the conquerors.

71 The Bhagavad Gita is said to be first narrated in 3138 BC during the Mahabharata war, according to the studies made by legendary mathematician and astronomer Aryabhatta, in 400AD during Gupta period. He based his dates on archaeo-astronomical methods.

American philosopher and author Henry David Thoreau (1817-1862), who read some portions of the Gita everyday, said: "In the morning I bathe my intellect in the stupendous philosophy of the Bhagavad Gita. In comparison our modern world and its literature seems puny and trivial".

In 7-2, the Gita states: 'after knowing this, nothing worth knowing remains to be known again'. Therefore, this knowledge is also known as the ultimate knowledge, or that knowledge that is most difficult to uncover Adi Shankeracharya has summed up: "From the clear knowledge of the Gita all the goals of human existence become fulfilled. The Bhagavad Gita is the quintessence of all the teachings of the Vedic scriptures".

Thus, the Gita yields a kind of knowledge that armed with it, one does not yearn for any other knowledge.

With What Purpose does One Read the Bhagavad Gita

What would be the benefit of reading the Bhagavad Gita? What would we gain?

Nothing except uplifting of self to a more evolved being, from human to better human and from better human to being divine, by showing us who we are, why we came into the being, what is the aim of life and what is the route to its fulfillment. We want to know about our true self. This knowledge will tell us how to improve our own self. Once we practise this knowledge, it will automatically help the world around us. The knowledge of the Bhagavad Gita is known as "Atma-Jnan" or "Knowledge of the Self" or the "Self-Realization", or simply the 'Spiritual Knowledge'. It can be further elaborated as the 'knowledge about me, my Creator, and the world that He created'.

No material benefit is promised. No heaven is promised to its readers, nor hell promised to people who ignore it. What matters is only the practice of what you are convinced about. Vedic Hindu traditions boldly say that the scriptures are to be learned for their own sake and not for any material benefit.

What to Look for When Reading the Bhagavad Gita

To be able to understand the Bhagavad Gita or for that matter any ancient Hindu text, the reader needs to know the purpose for which the text has been prepared. In the broad sense, all Hindu texts are meant for two basic purposes: Firstly, for the self- development, or more aptly, as Aldous Huxley has put it, for 'self-evolution' and secondly, for the sustained stability of the society. Stability is no less important as without that no individual can hope for any growth, whether that of society or personal. The Vedic sages had understood that everyone wants to develop and evolve. Our this desire is obvious and yet most of us are oblivious to it; that desire being dormant and as yet unmanifest (until one started to think about it). This is in fact our innate and intense desire. Therefore, each and every Vedic text, especially the Bhagavad Gita, tries to quench our that quest by showing the path towards evolution which ultimately culminates in the Realization of the Self.

The Gita, if studied with this perspective of self-evolution, as a guide for self-betterment, read with love for the subject and with respect for the purpose, will uncover profound truths for the reader. Hindus call it Self-Realization, Liberation or Mukti. If not so far as to the coveted 'Self-Realization', certainly it will make him a better human; make him at peace with himself and the world at large. But any other intention while studying the Gita will not do much more than fulfilling one's curiosity and will be a futile labor. We all know the proverbial boatman who sits in his boat and oars for the whole night, only to discover in the morning that his boat has not traveled even one inch because he had forgotten to release the anchor.

While it is important to know what to look for, it will also help know what not to expect in the text of the Gita. By conventional wisdom, most people tend to believe that the Bhagavad Gita would be somewhat similar in content to the holy books of other religions, such as Bible, Koran or Torah.

This belief can lead to directionless-ness and misunderstanding when one is trying to read the Gita. Do not expect any stories, miracles, commandments or code of conduct in the Bhagavad Gita. It deals only with evolution of an individual to reach as high a place as God Himself.

The Song from God

Its name, 'the Bhagavad Gita', simply translated, means, 'The Song from God'. It could be restated as 'The Song from the mouth of God', or also as 'The Song of the Divine One'. As the Bhagavad Gita is considered an Upanishad, it is also fondly known as 'Gitopanishad'. Sometimes the respectful adjective 'Shrimad' is added due to reverence felt towards its revealer and potent of revelation; the 'Shrimad Bhagavad Gita' meaning 'The Revered Song from God'.

The Gita has 18 chapters and each chapter has varying number of verses from a minimum of 20 in Chpater 12 and Chapter 15 to a maximum of 78 in the last Chapter 18. In total, however, the Bhagavad Gita has exactly 700 Sanskrit verses. Some verses are spoken by Dhritarashtra, some by Sanjay; some by Arjun but bulk of the verses are spoken by Lord Krishna.

Reject or Accept: The Freedom of Choice

The climax of Bhagavad Gita comes in the end, almost after concluding the profound-most revelations. Far from compelling Arjun to follow the instructions, Lord Krishna asks Arjun to reflect fully upon what has been told and take whatever path he thinks fit. Reject or accept; the choice is yours! Call it the boldness of Lord Krishna or call His confidence on the judgment of His listener, or call it freedom of choice.

If Emerson has celebrated this freedom, he is truly our hero. Ralph Waldo Emerson, it is said, had danced with joy when he read that stanza: "Thus has the wisdom, deeper than the deepest, has been declared to you, fully reflect this over and then act as you choose to act" (18-63). If the Bhagavad Gita has a special appeal among the intellectuals, it must be owing to this modesty, over and above the philosophic contents, the life principles, the spiritual aspects and the overpowering poetic-linguistic content. To imagine that Almighty God had patience enough to explain everything in fullest details, pouring himself out laboriously and meticulously, and yet, lo His preparedness to accept the choice of his 'student' when He grants him the freedom to accept or reject all the wisdom that has been unfolded. It is this freedom that separates the Gita from any other books.

Creator of the Gita respects the intellect of its reader and, therefore, though indicates the right direction; He does not pass any judgments on its reader nor gives any compelling commandments binding on them. A benevolent social reformer and author of one of the acclaimed treatise on the Bhagavad Gita, Vinoba Bhave said thus: "Hinduism gives its followers complete freedom. It does not insist on any particular discipline or prayer. Religion has to release us from bondage. The only imperative commandment it can have is to ask us to purify ourselves. Hinduism has emphasized the need for inner purity. Indian civilization and culture has shown a tremendous capacity for assimilation and absorption. If Hinduism becomes narrow, we shall be destroying our precious heritage."

The Bhagavad Gita and the Holy Texts of Other Religions

The Bhagavad Gita is not the 'Bible' of Hinduism. Except for the fact that the Gita is held in high esteem by most Hindus in the very same way the Bible is held by Christians, Torah by Jews and Koran by Muslims, there is not much similarities between the Bhagavad Gita and these texts.

DISSIMILARITY IN CONTENT

The Bhagavad Gita does not talk about the subjects that are discussed in Bible, Torah or Koran. It tells no stories, there are no miracles in it, it gives no moral codes, does not discuss the origin of the universe, history, heaven, hell or punishment for the disbelievers. Those subjects are discussed in many other

Hindu holy books such as the 'Manu-Smriti' and the 'Puranas', notably the 'Bhagawat Purana' and the 'Garud Purana'. Even these Hindu literatures too are different in their spirit, but are still somewhat comparable to the three Abrahamic holy books; Bible, Torah and Koran in terms of some of their contents.

The 'Manu-Smriti' gives the code of conduct, rules for the society, down from royalty to the smallest man, punishments, etc.

The 'Bhagawat Purana' talks about the beginning of the world, Heavens and Hell. Also it has numerous stories giving moral lessons and dos and don'ts, history, ten reincarnations of Lord Vishnu, cosmology with several symbolical illustrations of philosophical principles, genealogy of kings, and of their era.

The Garud Purana gives, among other things, the description of Hell, life after death, Karmic punishments, etc.

DISSIMILARITY IN REVELATION

The manner in which the Bhagavad Gita is revealed is qualitatively different from the revelations in holy books of other faiths.

The Bhagavad Gita was revealed by Yogeshwar Lord Krishna, God Himself. The revelation was not monopolized to one single person alone in seclusion but was fully heard and seen by more than one person. One of them was from Lord Krishna's side (Prince Arjun) and the other was from the enemy side (Sanjay, charioteer of Dhritrashtra). Thus the knowledge of the Bhagavad Gita was witnessed and corroborated by at least two independent individuals. The fact that both these witnesses were mutual enemies, lend to Gita an unprecedented credence. Additionally, the knowledge was revealed in broad daylight witnessed by thousands of soldiers on both the sides.

Although a dialogue between Lord Krishna and Arjun, the revelation is not restrictive in nature to only a certain class or certain religion-followers only. In its spirit and the content it speaks to mankind in general.

As for the Bible, it is believed that some part was revealed and some other was written with the divine inspiration received by several authors, approximately 40, from time to time. The Koran was revealed to Prophet Muhammad by Jibrial (Gabriel), the angel. Torah was said to be revealed to Moses by God.

DISSIMILARITY IN DURATION OF REVELATIONS AND PERIOD

The Bhagavad Gita is believed to have been revealed about 5000 years ago in a very brief time of perhaps a few hours.

Torah is believed to be revealed about 2800 years ago.

Bible (Old and New Testaments) is believed to be revealed between 1500 to 2800 years ago to different men over a period of approximately 1300 years.

Koran was revealed about 1400 years ago over a time period of about 23 years.

DISSIMILARITY IN VOLUME

The Bhagavad Gita is relatively tiny. It consists of just 700 verses. If one wants to chant it, one would easily do it in about two and a half hours. It is smallest among the books with which it is compared.

Torah has 5 books; they also form part of Bible.

Bible has 2 Testaments, 66 different books and totally 31,173 verses.

Koran has 114 Books containing about 6200 verses.

DISSIMILARITY IN THE NATURE OF THE SCRIBE

The nature of the scribes, their abilities, their personalities, their traits etc are generally unknown in case of some holy books. However, in case of the Bhagavad Gita, her scribe is a well known individual, an above board intellectual, a legendary leader, the

Lord Ganesh[72], famous as the 'elephant-headed God'. True to the word 'Ganesh' (Ganesh in Sanskrit means a 'group-leader', Gana=Group), he was the leader of Lord Shiv's Ganas. He is said to have scribed the entire volume of Gita totally uninterrupted when dictated by sage Veda Vyas, the author.

As for Bible, it was scribed over a long period of about 1300 years by several different individuals.

In case of Koran, the exact information about its all the scribes is not available, as it was dictated to various different scribes from time to time based on who was available at a given time, whenever the Prophet Mohammad, who was said to be illiterate, returned with revelations.

Almost entire Torah was scribed by Moses, however, its last part dealing with his death is said to be probably written by Joshua.

OTHER DISSIMILARITIES

The Torah is written originally in the Hebrew language, the Bible in Hebrew and Greek, and the Koran in Arabic. All these languages are widely spoken even now. The Bhagavad Gita was originally written in Sanskrit, which is not a language that is commonly spoken today. This makes it difficult for everyone, including Hindus to read it in the original.

Unlike any other holy texts, the Bhagavad Gita has exact date on which it was revealed, thus it is the only holy-book, whose birthday is celebrated every year, falling on the 11th Shukla of Margashirsh month of the Hindu calendar (Equivalent to November-December period). Devotees recite all 700 verses in one seating to celebrate her birthday.

Another important difference lies in the fact that the Gita does not show any 'chosen' or 'preferred' people or group

72 Lord Ganesh is son of Lord Shiv. He is considered as a deity who clears the hurdles in the path and is prayed to as the giver of intelligence.

for whom alone is the knowledge applicable. It talks about the liberation of the entire humankind, irrespective of their religion, colour or geographic location. Other texts apparently address only their followers, occasionally going beyond the followers to the 'people of the book', yet short of the whole mankind. Reference to the rest of the mankind in those holy books is mainly in terms of guidance as to how to treat them, how to tolerate them or how to fight with them. At places believers of other faiths are treated contemptuously in other holy books.

Pitfalls to Steer Clear of Misreading the Bhagavad Gita

At the eleventh hour, when war is about to begin, Arjun says to Lord Krishna that he does not want to fight his own relatives and that he would instead prefer to be killed weaponless, unresisting instead of winning and ruling the blood soaked land.

At 2-7 Arjun requests the guidance from Krishna: "My senses are overcome by the weakness of pity, and my mind is confused about duty (Dharma). Please tell me what is righteous for me. I am Your disciple, and I take refuge in You."

These sentences of the Bhagavad Gita taken in isolation from the rest of the Mahabharata may perhaps convey the sense that Arjun had a dilemma whether to fight or not to fight and that Arjun who did not want to fight was unnecessarily pushed into war by Lord Krishna and perhaps unfairly.

TO FIGHT OR NOT TO FIGHT? IS THAT THE CENTRAL DILEMMA?

It was a fight between cousins; both sides knew everyone on the other side; as relatives or friends. Viewed from Pandavas, side, 'to fight or not to fight' boils down to two different consequences. Fight will kill the relatives and friends but would uphold the truth and justice and punish the wrong-doer. Not to fight would although save the unjust relatives and friends from death but would mean submission to criminals. To save relatives from death is a familial personal duty and to uphold justice is duty towards the society. Both duties are valid whichever Arjun would have chosen. Arjun first chose his familial duty and then after listening to Lord Krishna he scrapped the familial choice in favour of more arduous duty towards the society.

Rephrasing above, it can be said that Arjun chose his Dharma towards the society instead of his personal familial Dharma.

This is precisely the reason why the Mahabharata war is described as the 'War for Fulfilling Duty' or 'Dharma Yuddha' and the Kurukshetra—where the fight took place is known in the Gita as 'Dharma-Kshetra.'

Many have misunderstood. They assume that 'to fight or not to fight', was Arjun's dilemma guided either by his better sense that war is bad on moral grounds or because Arjun was afraid of death. However, it would be misreading, if that is what is understood. Knower of Arjun's character does not need to be convinced that he, a veteran of many wars and planner of this war, would not discuss its morality at this stage or be afraid of death. In his life, he was never ever defeated in a war and who had experienced several brush with death during his life. It was neither morality nor morbidity of war that was behind the dilemma of Arjun. Arjun's dilemma was between two sets of 'Dharmas'. Two sets of call of duty.

During the Vietnam War, former US President Bill Clinton and former US Vice-president had refused to be drafted in the war-duty and several army personnel had refused active war-zone duty. Even during Iraq war similar instances were witnessed. They cited their conscience to stay away from war. They placed higher value to their personal duty borne out of their convictions than their duty towards state that was ordained by the majority in the US Congress. This is the conflict between two sets of duty.

Take the case of a devout Christian who has decided to follow "Thou shall not kill" based on the Ten Commandments. He will have a dilemma if asked to go to war-front, whether to follow his religious duty or his national duty. These dilemmas can be described as 'dharmic-dilemmas' and are sometimes confusing as to which duty should take precedence.

There was a survey[73] reported in the UK newspapers, done among British Muslims; how they describe themselves: Muslim first or British first? The overwhelming number preferred the former. Between two sets of duties, religious and national, which duty takes precedence?

The American constitution gives the individuals the right to freedom of conscience. The conscience is important and the choice is left to the individual. Same as what was done by Lord Krishna at the concluding part of the Bhagavad Gita, 5000 years ago.

Arjun had a dilemma. His one duty was to respect and protect his elders, friends and relatives. Another of his duty as a Kshatriya was to ensure and demonstrate that deceitful conduct does not pay, to prevent injustice from greedy and arrogant and to uphold truth. The former was his 'own personal familial duty' as a family member of the Kuru clan and the latter was his 'duty as a warrior towards the humanity, the world'. Arjun had to choose between these two 'duties' (Dharma). He preferred as confessed in the first chapter, the former. But by the time the entire narration of the Bhagavad Gita was over, he conceded that his earlier choice was out of confusion. It was more appropriate to look at the larger interest of upholding universal values of truth and justice even at personal loss and tremendous pain and inconvenience.

---

73 PEW Global Attitude Project, Report released on 7-6-06: What do you consider yourself first? 7% British Muslim respondents said 'British' and 81% Muslim responded saying 'Muslim' More details www.pewglobal.org the survey was done between 31-3-06 and 14-5-06.

This world is full of those jewels among men, who have chosen the call of higher duty in preference for other duties. Mahatma Gandhi's critics, his own son as well as his grandson included, have criticized him for ignoring the family welfare. Hermann Hesse chose to run away from the cherished goal of his parents to pursue his own conscience. In the ancient Indian context, Prahalad jumps to mind; he defies his father, Hiranyakashyap, the most powerful king of his time.

All good people take the 'Dharmic' (righteous) path but histories are made by those among the good, who take up the higher 'Dharmic' path in preference to other available weaker 'Dharmic' choice. It is all about your choices. Very simply but very powerfully 'Kath'-Upanishad (or pronounced together as 'Kathopanishad') in its summary would mean, there are basically and perennially just two choices before every person: "The 'Preyas' and the 'Shreyas'" ('Preya'='that which you would like' and 'Shreya'= 'worthy of fame-and-recognition'). Merely two choices! People choose between that which they 'like to do'; or that which they 'ought to do'.

Therefore in the Gita, Lord Krishna refers this war as 'Dharma Yuddha', the righteous war, the war between two sets of Dharma. Dharma Yuddha cannot be translated as 'religious war', a mistake some readers do, not knowing the difference between 'Dharma' and 'religion'. Dharma-Yuddha is neither a religious war nor a crusade.

BHAGAVAD GITA ADVOCATES WAR?

There are some who hurriedly conclude that the Bhagavad Gita advocates war. The apostle of peace, Mahatma Gandhi, who shaped his non-violent freedom struggle, could not have considered the Gita as his life-guide, if it really advocated war. The employment of non-violent struggle was unheard of until Mahatma Gandhi employed it against the British. His success has transformed the political struggles around the world ever since. Mahabharata supplies enough evidence to prove that both Pandavas and Lord Krishna did everything that could be done to avoid the war. Also from the first chapter of the Gita, it is clear that Arjun preferred not to fight; war-mongering was the last thing in their character. They desperately wanted to avoid the war.

In his poetry Four Quartet referring to the Gita, T S Eliot has given uncannily accurate message of the Bhagavad Gita: "Without consideration towards result, just fare forward, not fare well but fare forward". The Bhagavad Gita does not advocate the war but it advocates righteous action without caring for the consequences.

Swami Prabhupad's remark is useful to further understand: "On perusal of the first chapter of the Bhagavad Gita one may think they are advised to engage in warfare. When the second chapter has been read it can be clearly understood that knowledge and the soul are the ultimate goals to be attained. On studying the third chapter it is apparent that acts of righteousness are also of high priority. If we continue and patiently take the time to complete the Bhagavad Gita and try to ascertain the truth of its closing chapter we can see that the ultimate conclusion is to relinquish all the conceptualized ideas of religion which we possess and fully surrender directly unto the Supreme Lord."

Historic Krishna, Lord Krishna and the Yogeshwar Krishna

HISTORIC KRISHNA

Without knowing Krishna, the Bhagavad Gita can never be fully understood. He is the main actor in the drama of the Mahabharata. Minus Lord Krishna, the Mahabharata is lack-lustre. Krishna is a cousin of Pandavas. Vasudev, the father of Krishna is sibling of Kunti, the mother of Pandavas.

Krishna was 'Pramukh' (President) of 'Vrushni Sangh' (Federtion of States of Vrushni sect of Yadav dynasty). Vrushni Sangh was not an old fashioned kingdom, but was a modern federal republic, having elected chiefs (Presidents). This is the reason, although he ruled almost all his adult life, Krishna is never known as a 'king'.

Apart from being a legendary leader, who won many wars and brought wealth for his countrymen, he is more known as a statesman, a great leader, a knowledgeable person, and a dependable ally. Interestingly, he was generally not known as 'Lord' Krishna to the actors of Mahabharata, until he reveals His actual Self in the Bhagavad Gita to Arjun. He was more known as a cousin, a friend and a well wisher.

Lord Krishna was born inside a prison where both His parents were held by Kans, the king of Mathura, a city on the bank of river Yamuna, about 145 km south of Delhi. The rule of Kans extended to a larger area beyond Mathura. Krishna was smuggled out of the prison and was left with foster parents Nand and Yashoda in a small hemlet 'Gokul', across the river. Since his childhood, Krishna was a favourite of the village-folks. He spearheaded a movement among local milk-producers and cattle herders ensuring that people of Gokul had first right over the milk and butter produced by them instead of its wholesale export to neighbouring Mathura. While still a small boy, he led the people of Gokul to a safe passage to nearby village of Vrindavan in face of ravages of wild beasts and other calamities. He saved the new settlers in Vrindavan from fury of rain and flooding. There are numerous miraculous episodes in the life of Lord Krishna, all detailed in the 'Bhagawat Purana'. Even today monuments exist in the towns and villages lived in or visited by Lord Krishna which have become the sites of pilgrimages.

In the ancient India, the so-called 'modern' concept of 'a republic run by the people's representative' was not uncommon. Indeed there were many traditional kingdoms too in India. Ugrasen was the elected president of Vrushni Sangh. Their neighbouring state, kingdom of Magadh was ruled by a powerful king Jarasandh. To increase his political and economic clout, Jarasandh had cultivated friendship with Kans, son of Ugrasen, and even got his both daughters, Asti and Prapti, married to Kans. But Jarasandh knew that in the democratic republic, unlike a kingdom, there were no guarantees that president's son Kans can claim his father's throne. Should someone else come to power, Jarasandh would lose the advantages he had calculated to obtain from cultivating Kans, and even his daughters will not become queens. Therefore, he instigated Kans to revolt against his father, seize power, turn their republic into a kingdom and install himself as king. Kans liked the idea and putting behind bars his own father, he assumed powers.

Lord Krishna, now resident of Nandagaon, as an adolescent boy, was invited by Kans to compete with ferocious wrestlers with a motive to have him killed unsuspiciously in the sport. During the wrestling bouts, two of the Kamns' ferocious professional wrestlers got fatally injured and died in the arena. Kans who was watching the bout from a high seat in the stadium was shocked at unexpected turn of the event, not only failed to declare the winner but also insulted boy Lord Krishna and asked him to leave the arena. Unflinching, Lord Krishna walked up to the high chair of Kans, and challenged him to fight that kans accepted. Krishna killed kans in the wresthing bout. Thus ending Kans' life, he released the legitimate ruler Ugrasen from dungeon and restores his presidentship to the great relief of Mathura citizens.

In due course, upon Ugrasen's departure, Vasudev is chosen as president and thereafter Lord Krishna is elected president of Vrushni Republic. That Krishna had supernatural abilities and that the episodes of miraculous happenings around Him since His birth were generally known during that time, however, for Pandavas, he was more their cousin than a divine being. Especially to prince Arjun, He was his best friend and well-wisher, and much less a 'God'. The 'Bhagavan' (God) word was never used for Him until His revelation of the Gita. Even in the Mahabharata, Krishna appears at hundreds of places, but as an individual, a mortal Krishna, a Krishna perhaps with more abilities than an average person, but certainly not the God Krishna. In the Bhagavad Gita alone he is described as 'Bhagavan', meaning, the God.

Lord Krishna admired qualities of each Pandav brothers. Especially He had utmost respect for the eldest brother Yudhisthir, who would never speak untruth. Among all he loved Arjun the most due to his incomparable character derived from blend of strength, knowledge, humbleness and ever-prepardness to do the righteous things.

Weaponless non-combatant, Krishna accepts Arjun's request to become his charioteer. The Bhagavad Gita is the conversation that takes place on the war-ready chariot, between Lord Krishna and Arjun, minutes before the onset of the most terrible war, in which even nuclear[74]-tipped guided missiles were said to have been used.

BHAGAVAN (LORD) KRISHNA

Miracles started to happen from the time Lord Krishna was born till he ended his life. But all these were taken lightly by everyone including Lord Krishna himself. He appeared too small and too childlike to be instrumental in the happenings around him, although hundreds of miracles were witnessed by people of Gokul, Vrindavan and Mathura.

During the discourse of the Bhagavad Gita, Krishna reveals his identity as the Supreme Being, Creator, Sustainer and

---

74 Description of Brahmastra tells us that it had even more features than the current-day nuclear-tipped-guided missiles. Brahmastra could be called back by the sender if required before it hits the target. As per the Mahabharata, after the end of the deadly war, they decided that the nuclear weapons were truly very harmful and they destroyed the entire nuclear stockpile of the world.

Destroyer, the God. From the Chapter 1 to Chapter 10 it becomes progressively clear that the speaker, Krishna is someone more than the Krishna, the cousin of Arjun, or the son of Vasudev and Devaki. In Chapter 4, in the narration beginning from verse 5, Lord Krishna's real form as the God becomes evident, when He explains His reincarnation. Chpater 10 describes the essence of Almighty God, and unequivocally states at 10-37 that "He is Krishna among the Vrushni-Clan", clearly meaning that the speaker is someone more than Krishna. Whatever lingering doubts may have been, in Arjun's mind are dispelled in the Chapter 11, when Lord Krishna, reveals his true Self, when God actually gives a glimpse of His actual Self, never seen before by any human being, and impossible to be seen with normal human eyes, awfully frightening to Arjun. Even bravest of brave Arjun was unprepared to actually see the awful and fearsome cosmic form of God in its fullness. At the end of 11th Chapter, Arjun stunned, with words slipping out of his mouth spontaneously, says: "O' God, without realizing who you are, in my ignorance, I considered you merely as my friend, I ate, drank, slept, moved around and sat with you, I have joked with you, have called you names, may have insulted you in presence of others in my ignorance and arrogance, please forgive me." The discourse continues till 18th Chapter.

Thus the Bhagavad Gita is the sacred dialogue between God Himself and Arjun.

Because in the Gita the knowledge is given by the God Himself, all the words spoken by Lord Krishna are stated as "God said" in the original Sanskrit text. Hence in this book too the same format has been retained. (In this book, the word 'Lord Krishna' is used almost everywhere except in the actual translation of the Bhagavad Gita, where true to its text the word 'God' or 'Supreme Being' is used as and when required. The actual word used in the original Sanskrit version, is "Bhagavan" that is translated as God.)

YOGESHWAR KRISHNA

Having realized his friend, his cousin, Krishna to be God, Arjun addresses Lord Krishna as Yogeshwar at 11-4: "O Lord, if You think it is possible for me to see Your universal form, then, O Yogeshwar, show me Your immutable complete eternal form" and after first mention of God as Yogeshwar at 11-4, the expression is repeated several times in later Chapters.

Although most Hindus consider Lord Krishna as God, and no questions, some interpret Him a shade differently; divine indeed from His birth, but Lord Krishna is said to be in the God's or Supreme Being's full divine glory while narrating the Bhagavad Gita. This interpretation comes from some verses of the Bhagavad Gita, where the word "Yogeshwar" is used as an adjective to the word Hari[75] at 11-9 and along with the word Krishna at 18-75 and at 18-78. Thus 'Yogeshwar' word is not a replacement word for Hari or Krishna, but it suggests that 'Yogeshwar' who is Hari (God) in the form of Krishna is the narrator of the Gita.

In other words, one can also say that the Supreme Being Yogeshwar was present at the time of narration of the Gita in the form of Krishna and in the Bhagavad Gita, the term 'Yogeshwar' is used as equivalent to 'Almighty God' or more specifically' to mean 'God in His full Glory'.

Accusations on Lord Krishna

There are those who think that Krishna does not deserve to be held in as high esteem as the God. That he was a wily politician and a master manipulator. He is also accused of being a seducer, a womanizer, a war-monger, a self confessed killer of several individuals, a person rolling in luxuries, being arrogant, etc. In his childhood he harassed the town folks, he was stealing things and was speaking lies. At best, may be a leader but certainly not a God. And that how starkly different he is as compared to

75 Hari means Lord Vishnu, whose 9th incarnation is said to be Lord Krishna.

Jesus Christ or Lord Buddha, who have suffered and sacrificed so much in their lives. This notion questions the very authority of Lord Krishna to preach the Gita and be considered a God.

None of the accusations are correct, and are made either by the people who did not had the opportunity of learning more of Lord Krishna's character or by those who had ulterior motives. If one wants to go into the details of the historical account of Lord Krishna as a person, the reader is advised to read ancient text, 'Hari Vaunsh' or its translations rather than any second-hand material.Whatever be the accusations, those who belittle Krishna are unable to belittle his philosophy of the Bhagavad Gita. It remains the tallest.

At 7-24 and 7-25, in the Gita, Lord Krishna says: "The ignorant ones—unable to understand My immutable, incomparable, incomprehensible, and transcendental form—assume that I, the Supreme Being, am a form or a body. Concealed by My divine power (Maya), I do not reveal Myself to such ignorants who do not know and understand My unborn, eternal, and transcendental form and personality."

Attacks on the Personality of Lord Krishna

Lord Krishna's personality is a subject of mystery for many. And perhaps one can be pardoned for that view as Krishna had done so many different things in his life time, impossible for a single person in one life-time.

In his infant years, he is said to have playfully killed a couple of demons who were intent of killing Him under the order from Kamns. During his boyhood he is said to have been such a romantic personality that all the females, old and young of his village Gokul, were in 'platonic' love with him. He is further described as a mischievous boy-leader of children of Gokul who roamed the streets, stealing butter from the houses and feasting on it with his friends. In the Bhagawat Purana, Lord Krishna is described as a playful flute-totting cowherd. He is said to have led the local population to safety from several disasters. He is said to have been educated in the Ashram-School of a much respected sage, Sandipani. As a young warrior, he has fought many battles at several places from western India to far corners of Eastern India upto Assam and north east, as a politician he has advised kings and helped them to many alliances and treaties. As a philosopher he has said the Bhagavad Gita. As a mortal, he is said to have died in Veraval near Dwarka in Gujarat, hit by an arrow shot by an ordinary hunter who mistook Lord Krishna from distance to be a deer in the forest. He is said to have been a prolific wrestler, a politician, a statesman and a philosopher. Above all, He is said to be divine and the ninth incarnation of Lord Vishnu, the Sustainer.

During the last centuries the ranks that followed Max Muller and others who were keen to degrade and destroy the Hindu faith said 'it could not be one and the same person; surely there should have been many Krishnas', an argument aimed to belittle Lord Krishna. This view prevailed for sometime. However, this view is since discarded as all anecdotes of Krishna seem to be connected with the specific one Krishna, the son of Vasudev and Devaki.

In Puranas, there are stories involving thousands of wives of Lord Krishna. Apart from his eight wives (Rukmini, Satyabhama, Jambavati, Neela, Mitravinda, Lakshana, Kalindi and Bhadradevi), Lord Krishna is said to have married about 16,000 other wives. This is interpreted by some 'intellectuals' to be a proof that Lord Krishna was an immoral womanizer, maintaining a harem and could not be the creator of the Bhagavad Gita. The truth is far different if one was to understand Puranic accounts. Sixteen thousand women were enslaved by a brutal tyrant Narakasur[76] who had won many smaller kingdoms and had taken their kings and women-folk as prisoners. Lord Krishna, the Purana states, fought heroic

76 Narakasur was a powerful king of Pragyajyotishpur, who was eventually killed by Lord Krishna on 14-Krishna of Ashwini month.

battle, defeated Narakasur and had liberated imprisoned kings from the jail and women from harem. These liberated women were given protection by Lord Krishna from the society who would not easily accept those 'contaminated' females. Lord Krishna was a revolutionary. His solutions were revolutionary, different from ordinary; he is famed for 'tritiya-pantha' (Finder of a 'third' or an Unusual alternative).

From the followers of other faiths, another objection comes disputing Krishna as God. For a Muslim or a Christian, it is hard to imagine a living God intermingling with humans and living with them. This objection is somewhat understandable looking from their point of view that they do not expect living God, a God that takes birth and that dies like a mortal the way Lord Krishna (or for that matter Lord Rama) did. For Hindus that is not a problem, as they have always believed that God incarnates from time to time to guide the mankind. And also every human has the ability and potential for evolution from human to divine, making it possible for human to become God.

Names of Lord Krishna in the Bhagavad Gita

Lord Krishna is addressed variously in the Bhagavad Gita as Achuta, Madhav, Hrishikesh, Govind, Madhusudan, Janardan, Dev-Var, Adyam, Yadav, Kamal-Patraksh, Keshav, Bhagavaan, Bhagavan, Devesh, Parameshwar, Varshenya, Keshunishudan, Prabho, Vishveshwar, Purushottam, Devdev, Bhutesh Vaasudev, Vishno and Yogeshwar.

Repetitions and Contradictions within the Bhagavad Gita

Some readers have felt that the verses of Gita are repeatitive and are sometimes contradictory. Even Arjun had some confusion in this regards, until he had heard the entire message. He was a bold seeker and, therefore, unhesitatingly, almost brazenly he has asked Lord Krishna in first two verses of Chapter three: "If You consider that acquiring transcendental knowledge is better than working, then why do You want me to engage in this horrible war, O Krishna? You seem to confuse my mind by apparently conflicting words. Tell me; decisively, one thing by which I may attain the Supreme" (3-1, 2). Arjun indeed got his clarifications as he heard Lord Krishna through till 18 Chapters, in which at last he concedes that: "By Your grace my delusion is destroyed, I have gained Self-knowledge, my confusion is dispelled and I shall do as You said." at 18-73.

Careful analysis done by a serious reader does not reveal repetition or contradictions, perhaps visible at first sight.

Major Commentaries on the Bhagavad Gita

Fascination for the Bhagavad Gita has led hundreds of thinkers and philosophers to engage in its deeper study and write commentaries based on their individual insight into the subject. Even today, works of many luminaries are available for us to compare our notes with and share their experienced interpretations. Among them are: Adi Shankaracharya (788-820), Ramanujacharya (1017-1137), Madhavacharya (1238-1317), Vallabhacharya (1479-1531), Nimbarkaracharya (11th century, dates lost by historians), Madhusdan Saraswati (1525-1632), Saint Gnyaneshwar (1271-1297), Swami Shivanand (1887-1962), Mahatma Gandhi (1869-1948), Lokamanya Bal Gangadhar Tilak (1856-1920), Sarvepally Dr. Radhakrishnan (1888-1975), Sri Aurobindo (1872-1950), Swami Prabhupad (1896-1977), Paramhans Yoganand (1893-1952), Swami Vivekanand (1863-1902), Vinoba Bhave (1894-1982), etc.

Nobel Laureates on the Bhagavad Gita

HERMANN HESSE (1877-1962)

Herman Hesse, recipient of 1946 Nobel Prize in Literature, said: "The wonderful thing about the Bhagavad Gita is that an un-preached, experienced wisdom reveals itself as a helpful suggestion. This beautiful revelation, this wisdom of life, this philosophy which has blossomed out into a religion is that what we are looking for and need." Hesse was born into

Christian missionary family with his both parents working for Basel Mission in India. His parents wished young Hesse to study Protestant theology. When forced to study it, at the age of fifteen he fled from the Evangelist study seminar. Many years later he wrote to explain his fleeing. He thought the fulfillment of his parental expectations of becoming a Protestant theologist was, for him; "synonymous with the loss of one's personality". It was like being sold to a specific dogma. In 1914, just a month after the outbreak of the First World War, he wrote a poem titled "Bhagavad Gita". Hesse himself says about this "Indian poem"-as it is called in the subtitle: "This narration is the declaration of a man of Christian origin and upbringing, who left the Church rather early and who endeavoured to understand other religions, especially Indian and Chinese forms of belief. I tried to discover that which is common to all confessions and all human forms of religiousness and that which stands above all national differences, that which can be believed in and respected by all races."

ALBERT SCHWEITZER (1875-1965)

Albert Schweitzer a medical doctor who was awarded Nobel Prize in 1952-53 for his philosophical work, 'Reverence for Life'. He thought that western civilization was in decay because of gradual abandoning of its ethical foundation. Ethics, according to Schweitzer, is the compelling reverence towards each and every being to the 'will-to-live' as one does to one's own. The true philosophy begins with: "I am life that wants to live, in the midst of life that wants to live." He said: "The Bhagavad Gita has a profound influence on the spirit of mankind by its devotion to God which is manifested by actions".

T S ELIOT (1888-1965)

A poet, dramatist and literary critic, received the Nobel Prize in Literature in 1948. He studied Sanskrit at Harvard. Eliot's poem had a strong religious purpose and referenced Christianity in it, he being part of the Anglican Church. However, he was drawn to the Hindu philosophy with which he supplemented his Christianity. Eliot quotes from the Bhagavad-Gita, in his poems of "Four Quartets":

"The inner freedom from the practical desire

The release from action and suffering, release from the inner

And the outer compulsion, yet surrounded

By a grace of sense, a white light still and moving."

He is quoted: "Indian Philosophic thought is so inextricably mixed up with Indian religious thoughts ....Two years spent in the study of Sanskrit under Charles Lanman and a year in the mazes of Patanjali's metaphysics under the guidance of James Woods, left me in a state of enlightened mystification. A good half of the effort of understanding what the Indian philosophers were after—and their subtleties make most of the great European philosophers look like schoolboys—lay in trying to erase from my mind all the categories and kinds of distinction common to European philosophy from time of the Greeks".

ROMAIN ROLLAND (1866-1944)

French novelist, was awarded Nobel Prize for Literature in 1915. He called Gita as the Universal Gospel in his essays. He was very strongly influenced by the philosophy contained in the ancient Hindu literature. A friend of Rabindranath Tagore and Mahatma Gandhi, he narrates India in glowing tribute. He writes in his "Essay on Life of Swami Ramakrishna Paramhans" that: "If there is one place on the face of the earth where all the dreams of living men have found a home from the very earliest days when man began the dream of existence, it is India....For more than 30 centuries, the tree of vision, with all its thousand branches and their millions of twigs, has sprung from this torrid land, the burning womb of the Gods. It renews itself tirelessly showing no signs of decay."

Other Thinkers on the Bhagavad Gita

For thousands of years, the Gita has guided humanity. Readers have found deeper truths every time it has been read and newer truths everytime re-read. It has transformed the lives of millions of people. There are literally thousands, whose names should appear below, but only a handful are included; those whose names may sound familiar to the intended readers. It is not that following persons are endorsing the Gita on the lines a tooth paste is endorsed by some dental association. I have tried to reflect awe, sincerity and compulsion they felt towards a book that was completely alien to them till they came across it.

RALPH WALDO EMERSON (1803-1882)

Author, philosopher and poet, was born to the Rev. William Emerson, a Unitarian Church Minister in a famous line of ministers. Emerson however slowly drifted from doctrines of his peers. He was reading the Bhagavad Gita and Henry Thomas Colebrook's Essays on the Vedas. Strongly influenced by these oriental philosophies, he founded 'Transcendental Club'. His essay 'The Over-soul' exhibits his convictions of non-dualism. He once stated: "I owed a magnificent day to the Bhagavad Gita. It was the first of books; it was as if an empire spoke to us, nothing small or unworthy, but large, serene, consistent, the voice of an old intelligence which in another age and climate had pondered and thus disposed of the same question which exercises us."

MAHATMA GANDHI (1869-1948)

Undoubtedly one of the best known Indians, was imprisoned several times by the colonial British power, however, during one of the jail stints when he was held at Yeravada Jail in Pune, near Mumbai for leading freedom struggle of India, Mahatma Gandhi spent his time, just as done by Tilak, in writing commentary from his own unique perspective on Gita, the book that was most central to his life and thoughts. In his commentary, in Gujarati, he writes: "He who acts towards others as if they were himself will meet their needs as if they were his own, will do to others what he would do to himself, will learn to look upon self and the world as one." And no wonder he won everyone's hearts, of his friends and opponents alike. He not only read the Bhagavad Gita daily but also shared from what he read during prayer meetings that he used to hold, attended by hundreds on a daily basis. He further says on Gita that "it calls on humanity to dedicate body, mind and soul to pure duty and not to become mental voluptuaries at the mercy of random desires and undisciplined impulses".

LUDWIG VAN BEETHOVEN (1770-1827)

Ludwig Van Beethoven, German, among the greatest of music composers, was influenced by the older Hindu scripture, the Rig-Veda. In his diary he jotted down a line from the Rig-Veda commentary about the idea of God being "free from all passion and desire". He was attracted by Hindu thoughts as clearly attested by numerous passages and notes and fragments of Upanishads and the Bhagavad Gita found in the Beethoven papers, referring to the Indian ideas and texts. Beethoven was first introduced to Indian literature by an Austrian Orientalist, Hammer Purgstal, who had founded a periodical for the dissemination of Eastern knowledge in Europe.

ANNIE BESANT (1847-1933)

Annie Besant English social reformer, was born in London and died in India. She had worked closely with Mahatma Gandhi for India's freedom movement. Annie Besant was elected president of the Congress party for one year, however they split up when other leaders of the party appeared wedded more to the socialism, disregarding India's spirituality. Although not with the Congress party she still continued actively supporting Freedom Movement on the model of the Irish Freedom Struggle until her death. She was president of Theosophical Society and had written several books on Indian culture. Her English translation of Gita, "Bhagavad Gita—The Lord's Song" is considered by many as one of the best among available today. Some believe that even Mahatma Gandhi was first acquainted with Gita by that book. In 1895, Annie Besant made Kashi[77] her home and from there she started her own religious, educational and social services in India including the Central Hindu College, which was opened in 1898.

GEORGE HARRISON (1943-2001)

He was a song writer and a musician with Beatle group. A life-long devotee of Lord Krishna, he is said to read the Bhagavad Gita daily and held it in a very high esteem. In his songs, rather than use of heavy philosophical words, he preferred simple sing-along terms. In "Living in the material world" (1973), for instance, he sings: "Senses never gratified-Only swelling like a tide-That could drown me in the material world." The lines offer a terse rendering of several verses from Gita chapter two, which describes: "Delusion or wild idea arises from anger. The mind is bewildered by delusion. Memory is destroyed when the mind is bewildered. Reason and intellect is destroyed. With loss of memory and with destruction of intellect, one falls down from the righteous path" and as he thought "one falls down again into the material world."

CARL JUNG (1875-1961)

Carl Jung was a Swiss Psychiatrist, visited India. His experiences in India fascinated him with Eastern philosophies and religions, helping him come up with key concepts of his ideology, including integrating spirituality into everyday life and appreciation of the unconscious. When asked during a 1959 BBC

77 Kashi is also known as Varanasi from ancient times, somehow misspelled today as Benaras, or Banaras. All these names signify the same town Varanasi.

interview if he believed in the existence of God, Jung replied, "I don't believe-I know". On the Bhagavad Gita, with reference to 15-1, he commented: "The idea that man is like unto an inverted tree seems to have been current in bygone ages. The link with Vedic conceptions is provided by Plato in his Timaeus in which it states 'behold we are not an earthly but a heavenly plant'".

HENRY DAVID THOREAU (1817-1862)

He was an American author and philosopher stated: "In the morning I bathe my intellect in the stupendous and cosmogonal philosophy of the Bhagavad Gita, in comparison, our modern world and its literature seems puny and trivial", suggesting his daily reading of Gita, during his secluded simple living near the edge of Walden Lake.

WILHELM VON HUMBOLDT (1767-1835)

When Max Muller was belittling the Hindu literature, it was Wilhelm who was actively admiring and making it popular in America and Europe. Going even further, Wilhelm is also known for having made detailed study of the languages spoken in the Madagascar, whole of South-East Asia, from Malaysia to Philippines and beyond in Micronesia right up to New Zealand and has written on influence Sanskrit had on all these widely separated islands. On the Gita, he said: it is "The most beautiful, perhaps the only true philosophical song existing in any known tongue perhaps the deepest and loftiest thing the world has to show."

RUDOLF STEINER (1861-1925)

He was an Austrian philosopher and writer, described the Gita as 'Philosophy of freedom'. He has written and spoken incessantly on the Bhagavad Gita. He saw many parallels into the occult spiritualism of Bible and Gita. In the times when Eastern philosophies were very new to the west, he walked an extra mile to defend and explain them.

ALDOUS HUXLEY (1894-1963)

He is well known for his literary work, 'The Brave New World' where one sees the imprint of oriental ideas, said about the Bhagavad Gita that it is the "most systematic statement of spiritual evolution of enduring value to mankind. It is one of the most clear and comprehensive summaries of perennial philosophy ever revealed; hence its enduring value is subject not only to India but to all of humanity". Aldous Huxley wrote in the introduction to Prabhavananand and Isherwood's "Bhagavad Gita—Song of God": "The purpose of human life is the discovery of Truth, the unitive knowledge of the Godhead, Contemplation of truth is the end, action the means."

CHRISTOPHER ISHERWOOD (1904-1986)

Christopher Isherwood a British-American novelist and playwright, a disciple of Swami Prabhavananand, called himself Hindu and produced jointly with him one of the best known translations of the Bhagavad Gita. "Action rightly renounced brings freedom, action rightly performed brings freedom. Both are better than shunning of action...The wise see knowledge and action as one: They see truly. It is not aloofness and indifference to our actions or our lives that we wish to cultivate. Rather, we need to determine the most appropriate action and pursue it with vigour, while detaching ourselves from the results. He who does the task dictated by duty, caring nothing for fruit of the action, he is a yogi."

WILLIAM QUAN JUDGE (1851-1896)

William Quan Judge born in Ireland, settled in US, was co-founder of Theosophical Society in New York. When he died at the age of 44, he was well on his way to complete his 'Essays on The Gita'. Although the essay could not be finished; when the end came he had completed interpreting Bhagavad Gita till the 7th chapter. While on it, he emphatically stated: "but if the first two chapters of Bhagavad Gita were preserved, and the others lost, we would still have enough."

HENRY THOMAS COLEBROOKE (1765-1837)

He was an English Civil Servant in Colonial India. He learnt Sanskrit and translated many Indian books into English. He was president of The Royal Asiatic Society. His famous, 'Essays on Vedas' is cited as inspirational to many Western philosophers including Gita's most ardent admirer, Ralph Waldo Emerson. Colebrooke considered the Bhagavad Gita as his inspiration.

J ROBERT OPPENHEIMER (1904-1967)

The physicist who exploded world's first experimental nuclear bomb in the deserts of Nevada near Alamogordo on July 16, 1945, had himself studied Sanskrit language and had read Gita. Witnessing the explosion from his observation post on the site of detonation, when the bright lights of explosion flashed and the earth below shook to the loud noise, he uttered the verse 12th of Chapter 11: "If the splendour of thousands of suns were to blaze forth all at once in the sky, even that would not resemble the splendour of that exalted being." Years later in an interview, he mentioned that yet another verse also crossed his mind at the time he saw the explosion; he recalled the moments that elapsed after the explosion, in a 1965 NBC Television documentary that: "We knew the world would not be the same. A few people laughed, a few people cried, most people were silent. I remembered the line from the Hindu scripture, the Bhagavad-Gita. Vishnu is trying to persuade the Prince that he should do his duty and to impress him takes on his multi-armed form and says, 'Now, I am become Death, the destroyer of worlds.' I suppose we all thought that one way or another."

The list of Gita followers and admirers is truly very long. It includes many of the world thinkers, such as Albert Einstein (1879-1955) winner of Nobel Prize in Physics in 1921, EM Forster (1879-1970), An English Novelist, famed for his book, "Passage to India," George Orwell (1903-1950), author of "Nineteen Eighty Four" and "Animal Farm," Somerset Maugham (1874-1965) who visited India in 1938 and subsequently wrote his famous book 'Razor's edge' in 1944, its epigraph carries the famous Kath-Upanishad quote: 'The sharp edge of a razor is difficult to Passover, thus the wise say the path of salvation is hard" Other names to mention, Nicholai Roerich (1874-1947), William Digby (1849-1904), economist, Albin R. Gilbert, P.J. Saher, Will Durant (1885-1981), Col. H.S. Olcott (1823-1907), Helena P. Blavatsky (1831-1891), Jawaherlal Nehru (1889-1964), Rabindra Nath Tagore (1861-1941), William Butler Yeats (1865-1939), and Sylvain Levi. Rudyard Kipling (1865-1936), in his famous poem, "If,"describes the balanced man drawing close parallel to the steady man of Gita 2-54, 55, 56 and 57 "If you can meet with triumph and disaster and treat those two imposters just the same."

Dissenting Views on the Bhagavad Gita

There aren't many serious dissenters; whatever miniscule numbers do exist, are more on the external attributes of the Bhagavad Gita than on its main substance.

These dissentions can be classified in 4 categories:

1. Few scholars think that the Gita was written by somebody unknown (name not provided by the dissenters as yet), but introduced in the Mahabharata at a later date, for glorifying Lord Krishna. These dissenters do not dispute the content of the text but the revealer.
2. Some scholars doubt its date and would prefer it to be of 9th century BC, making it of about 3,000 years antiquity instead of 5,000 as believed traditionally. They too have no objection to the content of the Bhagavad Gita.
3. Some politicians and social workers have disagreement with the Gita only on account of one verse out of seven hundred; the one that deals with 'Varna-Ashram-Dharma' (the caste-system).
4. Total rejection of the Bhagavad Gita. This has come mainly from two leaders, Dr. Ambedkar and E V Ramasamy.

> Besides rejecting the Bhagavad Gita, they have publicly burnt 'Ramayana', that described the State of Ayodhya, fabled as utopian state, the 'Rama-Rajya' (The Kingdom or the Rulership of Lord Rama). Rama-Rajya was a dream of Mahatma Gandhi. He wanted India to be made into a Rama-Rajya. Its hallmark being a non-exploitative society, living in harmony; every citizen of Ayodhya living enlightened life based on service and duties.

MAX MULLER (1818-1883)

Max Muller was educated in Leipzig in Germany, where he learned Sanskrit and translated the 'Hitopadesh' of Pundit Vishnu Sharma before coming to England in 1846. In London, Max Mueller met Macaulay and was first commissioned by the East India Company to translate the Rig—Ved into English. The company agreed to pay the young Mueller 4 Shillings for each page that was ready to print. He later moved to Oxford where he translated a number of Sanskrit books. He is said to be the person having translated highest number of Sanskrit books. His biggest 'The Sacred Books of the East' is a grand 50-volume work. At one time, Max Muller appeared to have been a great service to Indian classical literature and was acknowledged thus by the Indian polity, however, in the hind sight, it was found that much of the translation was not accurate and was willfully made to mean something other than what was intended. He has although praised the Gita on occasions, his personal views were hardly favourable towards Sanskrit literature. Some believe that the translation was done firstly to earn money from the company and secondly to degrade the literature with a view to render it ridiculous in comparison with Christian literature, as visible from his own admission in his letters: "Large number of Vedic hymns are childish in the extreme; tedious, low, commonplace. I would like to live for ten years quite quietly and learn the language, try to make friends, and then see if I was fit to take part in this work, by means of which the old mischief of Indian priestcraft could be overthrown and the way opened for the entrance of simple Christian teaching…India is much riper for Christianity than Rome or Greece were at the time of Saint Paul….The rotten tree for some time had artificial supports but if the English man comes to see that the tree must fall, he will mind no sacrifice either of blood or of land...I would like to lay down my life, or at least lend my hand to bring about this struggle I do not claim for the ancient Indian literature any more that I should willingly concede to the fables and traditions and songs of savage nations."

In an audacious letter to N.K. Majumdar, Muller wrote: "Tell me some of your chief difficulties that prevent you and your countrymen from openly following Christ, and when I write to you I shall do my best to explain how I and many who agree with me have met them and solved them...From my point of view, India, at least the best part of it, is already converted to Christianity. You want no persuasion to become a follower of Christ. Then make up your mind to work for yourself. Unite your flock-to hold them together and prevent them from straying. The bridge has been built for you by those who came before you. Step boldly forward and you will find many friends to welcome you on the other shore and among them none more delighted than your old friend and fellow laborer F. Max-Muller."

DR BHIMRAO AMBEDKAR (1891-1956)

Dr Bhimrao Ambedkar a staunch opponent of Mahatma Gandhi, was British educated lawyer, architect of Indian Constitution and in India almost treated like a God for his work for the upliftment of lower castes. He hated the caste system, being its victim himself, and thought the best way to remove the system is to abolish Hindu Religion. At one time he thought of renouncing Hinduism and become a Muslim. But upon seeing that he will have to tow the line of Muslim clergy, he changed his mind and then became a Buddhist in 1956 and asked his followers also to get converted to Buddhism. Some followed but many didn't. It is reported by E V Ramasamy (1879-1973), that: "In 1930s Dr. Ambedkar told that he was thinking of becoming a Muslim. Mr. S.Ramanathan and I wrote to him: "Don't be in a hurry. At least a lakh of people should embrace Islam with you. Then only they will respect your ideas. Otherwise you have to follow what the Maulana says. Muslims say that their religion is a perfect one and as such there is no need to change it. When there is no scope for anything more than mere praying, worshipping etc, you will feel like imprisoned."

On one occasion, before independence of India when Dr. Ambedkar had come to Chennai, he said that "Bhagavad Gita was the blabbering of a lunatic". Sir C. P. Ramaswami Iyer had objected to this description of the Bhagavad Gita, stating that it was improper to express such views by the member[78] of the Viceroy's Council.

How bitter he was with Hinduism was evident from another of E V Ramasamy's dispatch: "Ambedkar has radical views about eradicating caste. They had in Punjab an Association (Jat-Pat-Todak-Mandal) to work for the abolition of caste. They had enrolled me also as a member. They asked Ambedkar to be the President of a Conference. Agreeing to their request, Dr. Ambedkar prepared his presidential address (Annihilation of Caste). It was sent to the organizers. They found in it, Ambedkar stressing the need to abolish Hinduism as a means to annihilate caste system. They wrote to him asking to remove that particular portion. They said that their association stood for eradicating caste and not for doing away with Hindu religion. But he pointed out that Hinduism was the basis of caste, and refused to remove the portion objectionable to them. He did not go to Punjab to deliver the speech. I got the address from him and published the same in 1936 as 'Jaathiyai Ozhikka Vazhi' in Tamil."

---

78 Between 1942 and 1946, Dr. Ambedkar was member of the 'Viceroy's Council', looking after equivalent of Labor Ministry.

Ramasamy further mentions that: "He (Ambedkar) severely criticized Gandhi for being an orthodox Hindu and for accepting Manu-Smriti and upholding Varna-Ashram-Dharma. He said that being an orthodox Hindu, Gandhi could not really do anything basic or substantial for the upliftment of Adi Dravidars[79].

In the words of Dr. Ambedkar himself: "I will not accept, hereafter, Rama, Krishna, Siva, Rudra etc. as gods. I do not believe in the concept of Avatara. I do not accept caste system, heaven, hell etc. I do not perform rites and rituals. I do not do Shraaddha[80] ceremony to my parents."

E V RAMASAMY (1879-1973)

E V Ramasamy an atheist, was an aggressively radical leader of 'lower-castes'. He consistently disowned Hinduism. In his words: "Following Dr. Ambedkar's conversion, media persons came to me. A reporter from Dhina Thanthi (a Tamil language daily) asked me if I would also quit Hinduism. I told him that there was no Hindu religion from which I had to quit. It has no founder, no head, no particular principle, not one authoritative scripture as in the case of Christianity, Islam and Sikhism. Those who believe and worship Rama, Krishna, Vishnu, Ganesh, Siva etc as gods and also those who hate them are considered Hindus. Theists as well as atheists are Hindus. Different people on different occasions, in different places have propounded different principles and practices which are opposed to each other. But these are all clubbed together under the generic term Hinduism which, as such, does not possess the essential

---

79 Adi-Dravidars, or original Dravidians, are said to be the inhabitants of the Indian subcontinent from very ancient times.

80 Shraaddha ceremony is a ritual done by a son or surviving members of the deceased person or persons. In the Hindu spirituality, Shraddha has a great spiritual significance for the dead and their living relatives and friends. It serves a very important role in the development of a man in terms of him becoming a grateful man, acknowledging efforts and sacrifices of the predecessors.

characteristics of a real religion. So there is no need for me and my followers to get converted." Ramasamy rejected all religions and remained away from the dogmas of all established religions.

How to Experience the Knowledge of Bhagavad Gita

The Bhagavad Gita is open to many interpretations, solely dependent upon the background of the reader. Different commentators have grasped different meanings, and they keep unfolding more meanings with every subsequent reading. One understanding leads to the other and thus deeper and still deeper meanings are understood. But the general rule is, more involved you are and keener you are more you will grasp. Educators have experienced this formula. Three pre-requisites for the maximum impact: Preparedness of the student, love for the subject and reverence for the teacher. The knowledge even if served on the golden platter will be wasteful on that student who is not well disciplined, who has not trained his faculties, who has no love for the subjects being taught and who has no respect for the teacher. Without these prerequisites, neither the university will be able to educate the student, nor will the student pick up the full potential of the knowledge.

No wonder the great teacher that Lord Krishna was, has stated at 18-67: "You should never disclose this science to one devoid of austerities, nor to the one who is not devoted, nor to one averse to spiritual advancement and never to anyone who is envious of Me". Initially I was haunted by this verse, when I thought of writing about the Gita, as how can I assume that every reader would have the attributes that Lord Krishna considered as necessary for proper grasping of the subject? Am I doing the exact opposite to the caution specified by Lord Krishna when I am presenting this book to every reader? After deliberations, I took upon myself to first raise the keenness of the reader for Gita by raising curiosity, stating many things normally invisible to a casual reader and making the reader look forward to the ultimate pinnacle of this subject matter, inspire reverence for Lord Krishna and then let reader in the end go into the translation. These steps are taken in best interest of the reader so that he gets maximum benefit from the Gita.

Arjun, the Ideal Student Who Received the Message

Arjun could get the full message from the Lord, because he was ready for it. He had all the three requisites. We want to be in his shoes, if we want to learn from the Gita. He learnt it perhaps in a few hours. We may take a bit longer, perhaps much longer, but it is not impossible. Arjun is admired by Lord Krishna due to his various qualities, evident from the way Arjun has been addressed in various verses by different names.

Arjun, from his childhood a keen learner, was always focused on his goal or target, was the best archer of his time and yet very humble. On the advice of Lord Krishna, he had taken up advanced studies in the field of Pashupatashtra (said to be a nuclear war-head tipped guided missile) from Lord Shiv and other powerful weapons after dedicated study of many years. He would never disobey his elders, whatever hardship he may have to undergo in its obeyance. He was so exemplary and so brave that even the enemies in the opposite camp had respect for him. He had the distinction of never having lost a battle in his lifetime, winning him a new name 'Vijay'. Arjun is also known by a name Jishnu, as he never used unfair means in the war. He had an impeccable character; during his studies of advanced weaponry, a legendary beauty, a nymph from higher worlds, Urvashi[81] lost her heart to him. Uravashi, apart

81 Uravashi, enraged by her rejection by Arjun, is said to have used her special powers to curse Arjun that he would never in his whole life be able to enjoy a woman (making him a defecto eunuch). However even such a terrible curse could not frighten him into submission to her advances. (This curse was later reduced to 12 month period at the intervention of Lord Indra. Arjun acturally found this curse helpful in dealing with his task of remaining hidden from Kauravs; thus using even her curse, profitably in the course of his life when living in the kingdom of Virat.

from being an exceptional beauty, was intelligent and the best dancer in the court of Lord Indra. Even she could not entrap virtuous Arjun, who was focused on his mission of study and return back to his family; he refused her advances. Arjun was not given to any temptations. In another episode, when approached for marriage by King Viraat, father of a young and extremely beautiful Uttara[82], he declined the offer respectfully. Despite his valour, he was not power hungry, his valiant fight in the war of the Mahabharata was not for becoming a king, the king would be his elder brother Yudhisthir, but he fought the war as his Dharma, his duty. And after the win, he helped Yudhisthir rule for many years until ultimately all the five Pandavas decided voluntary retirement and went to Himalayas for giving up their bodies (for dying).

Arjun had a dilemma and it was resolved. Almost at the end of God's narration Arjun has been given a choice to accept or reject it. Arjun, back from his confusion, says to Lord Krishna, unequivocally that his dilemma has been resolved and that he would do exactly as what Lord has said.

Arjun is the hero of the Mahabharata and also our hero. Just as he had questions, we too have many questions. In that sense Arjun is our representative. He has asked questions to Lord Krishna on our behalf; and therefore let us intensely follow their dialogue to uncover the ultimate knowledge.

Names of Arjun in the Bhagavad Gita

Parantapa, Gudakesh, Kuru-Shrestha, Parth, Dhananjay, Vijay, Jishnu, Pandav, Mahabaho, Kaunteya, Bharat, Kurunandan, Bharatarshabh, Kurusattam, Kurupravir, Anagh, Bharatsrestha, Bharatsattam, etc.

82 Princess Uttara was married to Abhimanyu, son of Arjun.

4

The Messages from the Bhagavad Gita

Even if a thousand messages were listed in-here, they would still be inadequate and still be trivializing this divine creation that is providing guidance to literally millions of habitants of the world enriching their own and other's lives. Experts on the Gita have delved on every single word of each verse, yielding thousands of messages for human uplifting. However, from the narrow perspective of an ordinary mortal, living an average life, a typical citizen of this world, I consider the following messages to be helpful in leading my day-to-day life with more satisfaction; inner as well as outer. They are primarily for one's own as well as societal evolution and not for 'making God happy' or for 'peace in heaven' or for getting wealth or any material boon. What attracts everyone is the fact that they are neither obscure sermons nor forced commandments but are logical deductions that anyone from across the world can apply and benefit and still live his normal life whatever be his faith or conviction.

Messages covering spiritual insights, Soul, Atma, Paramatma, Maya, Triple-tendencies, Equanimity, Mukti, Liberation, God-ness, merging with God etc, are omitted here being out of the scope of this book. They are important to advanced student of the Bhagavad Gita. He would know that these are the kind of things that are desired, nay demanded by our inner self, whether obvious to us today or oblivious to us today. In the ultimate analysis, all our wants narrow down to one single want, the want of Liberation.

1. OPTIMISTIC OUTLOOK: Gita makes me an incorrigible optimist in all the situations, however challenging or even grave they may appear. They are my opportunity for experience and researching; and, therefore, for my own progress. I am in this world for my own self-development. I want to reach the stage of a fulfilled person. (6-40, 41, 42, 43)
2. CONSIDEATION FOR OTHERS: I exist due to the mercy I experienced from others since my birth. I am not alone; I must share with others. Every one is my partner, to consume without sharing amounts to misappropriation and stealing. (3-12, 13)
3. LEARN LIFELONG: This world is a big school for education and experience and I want to be a fast learner; every situation, favorable, unfavorable or outright repulsive, in my life, is an opportunity of learning and improving my reaction. Knowledge of the Gita helps me remain a life-long student since no effort is wasted (2-40). I must relentlessly work on myself till my very end (death) (2-18, 40, 3-23, 24).
4. UNAFRAID OF DEATH: Spirit is neither born nor destroyed (2-18), therefore, death should not frighten me. I wish to live as long as possible giving me maximum opportunity of learning. I do not want to die but when death comes, I am ready to welcome it. Death is not to be feared as my learning will not be wasted and surely it would be carried with me to my next destination with even better opportunities.
5. LEADER TO LEAD BY EXEMPLERY LIFE: Leader should set example (3-21, 22, 23). Every individual is a leader somewhere, be it work, play, family, politics or any organization. My life should be exemplary.
6. SOLACE: God is not just up there; He lives in my heart with me. With divinity so close to me, watching over me,

gives me optimism and hope when difficulties arise. I know that even if the whole world was to abandon me, He would still be with me and will never abandon me. This knowledge gives me solace. (15-07, 15-15)

7. STOPS ME FROM MISBEHAVING: His being in my heart, watching over me also makes me feel more responsible in my behavior. I should not misbehave lest it be disrespectful to God. It teaches self-restraint. (15- 15, 12-13, 14)
8. GIVES SELFESTEEM: God's proximity with me fills me with a sense of proud self-esteem. It convinces me that I am not some faceless unwanted person. It awakens my spirit helping me become better evolved, worthy to His proximity by doing the deeds that can make Him feel proud of His trust in me of having chosen my heart to reside in. (13-15)
9. MAKES ME REASONABLE WITH OTHERS: God residing in my heart makes me humble enough to be reasonable with others, even when I am in a strong position; because I know that God is in the heart of others too. This knowledge saves me from doing damage to others even if I may have the capacity to. (13-15).
10. REMOVES MY HELPLESSNESS: His proximity convinces me that I couldn't be the helpless 'sinner' needing someone else to get me to Salvation. My Salvation does not depend on the 'mercy' of others. My Salvation is in my own hands by my own Karma, my own resolve and actions. (6-5)
11. GIVES ME CORRECT PERSPECTIVE OF WORK AND ITS RESULT: To work or not to work is in my hands. But I know that even 'not to work' is also a kind of work in the Karmic world. Thus the true sentence should be written as, I can only work, that is my only ability or say, is my only nature. I would surely be rewarded for

the work done. However, rewards of the work depend on many factors over which I do not have much control. Therefore, although I cannot escape working, I will work fully convinced that I have no control over its reward, it is a fact of life. At 2-47, it clearly says: 'You have control over doing the work but have no control over the result. Do not be desirous of the fruit of work nor remain inactive'.

12. SAVES ME FROM DISAPPOINTMENTS AND ANGER: My job is to work as diligently as possible and surely I would be rewarded, but I cannot expect any specific reward. This knowledge saves me from brooding on the result while working; thereby my concentration on working is more intense. Additionally, it saves me from falling to the depths of disappointment when the result is not as per my desire. (2-49, 3-19, 22)
13. MAKES ME ENVIRONMENT FRIENDLY: I must selflessly help proper maintenance of nature by doing things that can help proper rain, proper air, proper vegetation etcetera and those forces will in turn nourish me. It makes me a Go-green environmentalist; God has created everything. It is His world; not mine. Being His son, I should protect this world; not abuse it. World is not for me, I am for the world. I am not the master of the world. A follower of the Bhagavad Gita should be the best environmentalist. (3-11 to 3-14),
14. SAVES FROM FATALISTICISM: I am not helplessly tied to my fate. I can change my fate with my Karma. (18-14)
15. BALANCED LIFE: I should be balanced in my life; not eat too much nor eat too little. Not too much work and nor too little work; neither too much sense gratification nor renouncing all sense gratification. Life is for a balanced all-round development. (6-17)
16. GIVES HOPE AND ASSURANCE: If under utterly desperate situation, despair not, the Bhagavad Gita

comforts me by saying that God comes and will keep coming whenever required to protect righteous men and to control the unrighteous ones. (4-07, 08)

17. GREED CONTROL: There is nothing for free in this world. I should work for everything and not expect freebies. Freebie taken will have to be eventually paid up; so beware, that is what Karma doctrine is. This controls my greed.
18. VACCINATION AGAINST TERRORISM: Terrorism? No-No, I know that God has created everything and everyone; be he Hindu, Muslim or Christian; be he black, white, brown or yellow, he is as important as me. I will respect him, because I am convinced by the Gita that God resides in him, providing me with a logical reason to love my neighbor as me, he does not need to share my ethos, religion, country or language. Whatever and whoever is my neighbor is worthy of my love. I respect him as I do to myself. I will not enforce my agenda on him. This knowledge provides genuine world peace, not the lip service. (6-29, 32, 13-28)
19. NOT GOD FEARING BUT GOD LOVING ATTITUDE: God is merciful, why otherwise He sustains me? If I surrender everything to Him, He has guaranteed to look after my well being. (18-66)
20. RESPECT FOR OTHERS: I must have genuine respect for others on same lines as myself. (6-29, 30, 31,32) If my self dignity is valuable so is other's, and no-excuses. I do not want to belittle anyone nor do I want to be belittled by anyone. I do not want to kill and I do not want to be killed. This is true nonviolence. I will not humiliate others but also I will not accept self-humiliation, which is same as slow-poison that will kill my inner self.
21. COME WHAT MAY, DO THE RIGHT THING: Do the right things. I will fight for justice and fairness; it is my

duty; whatever are its consequences. Consequences are unimportant for the true seeker. I must fulfill my duty as whatever I am, a son, a father, a teacher, an employee, a government officer, a soldier or whatever even if it is hard to perform. (3-35, 18-47)

22. STUDY OF SELF, OF CREATOR AND OF CREATION: The study of the self, the Swadhyay, is the most important of all the studies; the Gita gives me insight into my own self. It tells me about the true nature of the world, it tells me about the nature of my creator, and step by step it guides me to evolve to be able to reach my creator.
23. FREEDOM OF CHOOSING METHOD OF WORSHIP AND DEITY: Verses 7-21, 22 unequivocally declare freedom of worship and choice of deity. No deity is inferior or worthy of my contempt. Verses 13-28 states that there is one and the same God in equal proportion in all the beings, hence no one should be harmed just because he worships a different deity. This strengthens my brotherhood feelings for others.
24. ABSOLUTE FREEDOM: The Gita trusts me and respects my free-will and lets me decide my own course of action. In return, it does not even expect a 'thank-you'. Where else can I find this freedom and this level of mature guidance? (18-63)
25. WORK IN THE SPIRIT OF WORSHIP: The Gita shows a clever way of doing my daily chores and activities in a way that my day-to-day normal activities get sublimated and get converted into God's service or self-less work. It shows the trick of transforming me from a mundane worker a real seeker or a worshipper while still doing my daily routine. With the unfolded secrets of how to achieve Liberation, the Gita provides easy, yet an accurate tool.
26. BEST ACTIVITY: What work can be better than the work that changes a man to become a better man? The food

charity will feed, medical charity will cure, education charity will help get a job, however none guarantees that beneficiary becomes a good son, a good husband or a good citizen of the world. But Gita inspired unique thought-action-love-'charity' (or 'non-charity') of Swadhyay, established by Pandurang Shashtri provides best hope as it heightens awareness of God's proximity, constantly raises the bar and ups human goodness progressively. The best work that I could do is to raise awareness of Gita which inspires and would help transform person of every denominator to become good. (18-68)

27. SELFLESS WORK LIFELONG: I must do selfless work using my body, my intellect, my mind and my wealth, throughout my life (4-25, 28) With wants sublimated, unhappiness is gone. I can reclaim my original self, as described in Vedas, as an embodiment of Bliss.
28. QUALITIES TO HANKER: Divine Qualities that I should appreciate are: Fearlessness, Purity of mind, perseverance yog of self-knowledge, charity, sense restraint, self-less-service, austerity, non-violence, truthfulness, absence of anger, renunciation, equanimity, abstaining from backbiting, compassion for all creatures, freedom from greed, gentleness, modesty, absence of fickleness, splendor, forgiveness, fortitude, cleanliness, absence of malice and absence of vanity. (16-1 to 3)
29. QUALITIES TO DISCARD: Qualities that I should discourage are: Hypocrisy, arrogance, vanity, ego, anger, harshness and ignorance. (16-4)
30. EVEN SINNER IS A POTENTIAL SAINT: I am a sinner, so what, it is also my learning to identify my mistake and that helps me to resolve to do the right thing. There is no doubt, I would be still attain salvation (9-30) and even be known as saint thereafter.

It is not difficult to see that the above messages will work towards self-development as well as the societal development. However it amounts almost to a 'Big Exposé', that none of the messages pre-suppose one to belong to any special race, religion, color or nation; none demands any rituals, pledges, undertakings, payments, taxes, hatred to anyone, proving that others are wrong, enrollment into a church or a temple etc. Quite to the contrary, it is an open-arm welcome to every human being as he is, at his own speed and at his convenience, an auto-pilot code of conduct that self-rejuvenates us and the world around us, without needing any artificial props. No wonder, wise men call the Bhagavad Gita, the Bible of Humanity.

All thoughtful people of the world are in search of solutions for the problems facing the world. It is a challenge. It is posed by consumerization, terrorism, global financial crunch, global warming, HIV[83], drugs, WMD[84] and their proliferation, wars, man made floods and famines, human trafficking, poverty, hunger, diseases, cartelization of oil, grains and other commodities, religious intolerance, suicide bombing, alienation, pornography, child-pornography, single mothers, breaking up of families, domestic violence, crimes, unemployment,...the list is endless. It seems, no one country or one individual can solve these problems; even jointly too it looks nearly impossible. Evils in the society manifest in various different ways but their roots cause, summed up spells 'uncontrolled human tendencies'. We want a system that can save us from impending disaster.

Want to solve the problem before it is created. Can we?

Do not be surprised if your thoughts too converge on the Bhagavad Gita and Sanatan Dharma.

---

83 HIV /Aids a deadly disease, Human immunodeficiency Acquired Immunodeficiency Virus

84 Weapons of Mass Destruction, such as Nuclear Bombs.

Index